The Pain Didn't Kill Me

MY STORY FROM THE HEART

[A MEMOIR]

DAPHNE BELL

THE PAIN
DIDN'T
Kill
ME

MY STORY FROM THE HEART

[A MEMOIR]

LUMEN-US PUBLISHING
BRINGING LIGHT TO THE MIND

Like one's concept of God, there is nothing more individuate than pain. It has its own idiosyncratic quality. Daphne expresses her victories over pain so powerfully, it definitely assuages the pain we feel.

—BISHOP NOEL JONES
City of Refuge Church, Gardena, CA.

I have known Daphne Bell for over 20 years; but I did not know her pain and her struggles. I applaud Daphne for her courage to allow me into her life and to walk in her shoes. This book inspires me to look at many facets of my own life: my past, my marriage, my children, and my health. Thank you Daphne for listening to God's voice. You are being used to heal the heart of others spiritually, emotionally, and physically.

—CRIS CARTER
Former NFL Player

Powerful writing ... Daphne Bell captured it in one sentence—what Todd didn't know cost him his life. She chose to tell this story so that someone else might avoid a similar fate. It is a story of sadness and loss, but also one of hope and optimism. Her message is that you shouldn't be afraid to go to the doctor—you should be afraid not to go. Most heart disease can be prevented. *The Pain Didn't Kill Me* is one very passionate writer's attempt to help others learn that simple lesson.

—THOMAS RYAN, M.D.
Director, The Ohio State University Heart Center

Daphne Bell's memoir is indeed a testament to what a loving couple can do for others. Daphne is truly a difference maker. She has passionately taken on the cause of heart disease awareness. Todd Bell is one of the great legends of Ohio high school athletics, as well as Ohio State football. Todd's impact was remarkable on the football field and continues to be at the Ohio State University's *Bell Resource Center for the African American Male*. *The Pain Didn't Kill Me* is a must read.

—JIM TRESSEL
Head Football Coach, Ohio State University

This is an awesome book that Daphne has written. Daphne has opened herself to help those who will read her story. It is a must-read for anyone who has ever gone through pain, hurt, disappointment, and feelings of being alone.

—**KEITH BYARS**
Former NFL Player

I immersed myself in the pages of Daphne's life story: her pain, her heartache, and her triumph. I'm surer now than ever before that "many are the afflictions of the righteous, but God delivers him out of them ALL." Daphne's story is a testament to that statement and also the fact that no matter what Satan throws in our path, and no matter how much more we don't think we can take, God has our back and He knows the way that we take. *The Pain Didn't Kill Me* will be a healing salve for many.

—**PATTI WEBSTER**
Founder/President, W&W Public Relations

Daphne's work to promote heart health awareness is a tribute to Todd's life. Her story courageously personifies the perseverance of the human spirit. Todd was taken from us much too soon. His time may have been short, but he led a very full life. He touched so many people and truly made a difference in this world.

—**ARCHIE GRIFFIN**
President/CEO of the Ohio State Alumni Association

When you journey with Daphne through the depths of her soul, you'll be amazed at her resiliency and resolve. Heartbreak and setbacks in her life made her dig deeper and press on in the Lord. She is living proof that what didn't kill her only made her stronger. My friend, Todd Bell, would be so proud of his wife if he were still with us.

—**MIKE SINGLETARY**
Head Coach, San Francisco 49ers

Daphne's message will create awareness of heart disease for everyone. Her compassionate and transparent story of her personal pain and triumphs will help and bless her readers. Being a friend of Daphne and Todd made us better people. The times Todd, Daphne, Reggie, and I spent together will always be joyfully remembered in my heart and mind. Daphne is a caring and compassionate woman; her direct challenge through her words can save many lives.

—**SARA WHITE**
Widow of Reggie White, NFL Hall of Famer

The Pain Didn't Kill Me indeed captures the essence of the time-tested hopes and promises of the American family . . . wrought with the harsh and stark realities of *Good Times* and replete with the traditional values of the *Huxtables*.

—**MARILYN FOSTER**
President/CEO, Lumen-us Publishing

The Pain Didn't Kill Me is a must-read. Through Todd's athletic record, we who worked with him at OSU were in contact with a tradition of dedication, excellence, and integrity. Todd showed us what a disciplined life could accomplish ... with his continuing dedication to physical and spiritual health. When Todd spoke, there was a power in him, a force that came from more than his athletic and academic accomplishments. Todd was a man committed to education and excellence. The world is a better place for his having traveled here.

—**MAC STEWART, PH.D., VICE PROVOST**
Office of Minority Affairs, Ohio State University

Daphne sounds the *blues* trumpet of personal tragedy with the surviving improvisation of *jazz*—orchestrated by the perpetual hope of a *gospel spiritual*—indeed a prescription for the existence of a people. Her song: *The Pain Didn't Kill Me*. Its verse: What you don't know can kill you; what you find ... may be your life.

—**JOSEPH A. WOODS**
Writer /Poet Laureate

FOREWORD
MIKE SINGLETARY
Head Coach, San Francisco 49ers

Friends for life. This phrase carries an implication of elderly adults sharing life experiences full of laughter and great memories. Never did I imagine that my friendship for life with Todd Bell would last only two and a half decades.

In the summer of 1981, Todd and I were rookies on a Chicago Bears team that had mastered the art of losing games. The physical and psychological demands of minicamps and training camps for an NFL rookie can be overwhelming, so it was a relief to find a teammate with whom I had so much in common. Todd, the son of a preacher, was a hard-hitting, soft-spoken man of few words. Both of us were careful with our paychecks, so we decided to room together in order to minimize our expenses. We actually had a third friend who was also a hard-hitting, soft-spoken man of few words. He is Leslie Frazier, but Les married his wife during the *bye week* of our rookie year. My girlfriend (now wife) was completing her studies at Baylor University, which left me with quite a bit of time to spend with Todd. If I wasn't at practice or watching film, I was hanging with Todd.

The funny thing about certain male friends is that there isn't always much need for conversation. There were many evenings around the apartment that I spent on the phone in my room, while he was on the phone in his room, and there was no angst about it at all. Yet there were plenty of other evenings that we spent hanging out in the living room, conversing over a television show or movie. Before I got married, I was adamant about my wife understanding that I liked to have time alone, and I wanted confirmation from her that she didn't expect me to become chatty and outgoing all of a sudden. Todd and I discussed this kind of stuff at length, like how we weren't really willing to change just because we got married. We had it all figured out . . . until I actually walked down the aisle and said, "I do."

I had been married for several years before Todd met Daphne. After I got married, my relationship with Todd wasn't the same as it had been when we were single guys. Todd was very respectful of my time, knowing that I was trying to become the kind of husband that we had both talked about being. But it didn't take long for me to recognize that some of our ideologies just didn't hold up in a real-life marriage.

Our dogmatic approach to being the head of the household was tried and tested in my home, resulting in the realization of a need for compassion and compromise to make my marriage work. During the time that Todd was still single after I got married, I sensed he felt maybe I had gotten "soft," and that I wasn't as tough as we'd talked about being. He never said as much to me; but like so much that passed between us, I just knew.

When Todd called to tell me he was asking Daphne to marry him, I heard a joy in his voice that he usually tried to keep hidden. He was quite guarded about his emotions, but he couldn't hide his excitement about marrying Daphne. I was so happy for him.

We spoke randomly and inconsistently over the next couple of years. I sensed that he was also holding on to some of the dogmatic ideologies of two young bachelors who hadn't a clue about how to treat a godly wife, and that his unwillingness to compromise may have been causing problems for their marriage.

A very small percentage of us get to plan our final days on this earth, preparing loved ones, saying the unsaid, and having final wishes granted. Todd's sudden and premature death caught all of us off guard. The flurry of activity preceding his funeral along with the rearrangement and reprioritization of schedules, made me keenly aware of my own mortality. Those times in life usually do. But I can't help but think that if I had the opportunity to join Todd for an evening in his apartment in heaven, just the two of us, that there would be plenty of conversation. I think he'd tell me that he regrets holding on to his emotions so tightly, especially with Daphne. I think he'd tell me to express my feelings openly, every chance I get. But I think his most urgent message would be to confirm what we both already knew: that a life with Jesus is the only way to live. He'd want everyone to be assured that they will spend an eternity in heaven with Jesus, but he'd also want us to live and love the way Jesus did while we're here on Earth. He'd want to remind me that when it's all said and done, love is what really matters. And he'd want me to make sure Daphne knew that he really, really loved her.

Daphne is someone I've grown to respect over these years since Todd's passing. She is a woman of strength: strength in character, strength in resolve, and strength in the Lord. When Todd and I sat around and discussed the qualities we wanted in a wife, he almost nailed it. Almost. Daphne far exceeded his expectations. That's just how God is ... He gives you more than you can imagine.

The Pain Didn't Kill Me
My Story from the Heart
Daphne Bell

ISBN 10: 1-936405-00-8

ISBN 13: 978-1-936405-00-8

Barcode: 9781936405008

First Edition

All Bible quotes are taken from the King James Version,
New Centruy Version and the New King James Version.

Editor: Joseph A. Woods, President, The Write Style Media Group
Photographer: Shellee Fisher Davis
Makeup Artist: Mikah D.M. Brown
Cover by: Divyne Designz

Lumen-us Publishing
Bringing Light to the Mind
www.lumen-us.com

Printed in the United States of America

I dedicate this book

To the unbinding inspiration of my husband, Todd

And

To the unfolding mystery of my family history

For without them

I would not have discovered ...

Me

CONTENTS

PART 4

EPILOGUE

RESOURCE GUIDE

ABOUT THE AUTHOR

ACKNOWLEDGEMENTS

Darkness greets me . . . my alarm clock, set as always for 3:30 a.m., jolts me. My internal alarm begs to differ. And the light of dawn that usually cheers early-morning commuters eludes me.

It's five o'clock in the morning and the start of my day as a morning drive-show news anchor and radio personality for *Radio One Columbus*. I enjoy my job. My co-hosts are like family to me. I serve as Public Affairs Director for our station, and I love it. It affords me the opportunity to meet and develop lasting relationships with our community leaders. Community service requests pour in weekly. If I don't check and clear my voicemail daily, it would fill up by the evening. I listen to every message; but I can't say that I return all the calls.

Because I'm on the air every day, listeners feel like they know me personally. Along with requests to host or emcee community events, I receive countless invitations to attend family reunions, weddings, and graduations. Of course, some things touch me differently than others—and the touch of some things moves me more than others.

I'm asked to deliver a speech for the African-American Healthy Heart Luncheon, hosted by the Coalition of 100 Black Women. I am quite aware that heart disease is the number 1 killer among women. And most importantly, I feel that this disease is not in the forefront of our minds. It doesn't receive enough media exposure.

I accept the invitation. I welcome the opportunity to help create awareness about heart disease because it relates to all women, and we should all be concerned. The organizers of the luncheon don't mind that I can't stay long; I promise to do my thing and then leave. They're just delighted that I can make it.

One month later on February 23, 2005, during *Go Red Month*, I stand here speaking before a sea of black women in solidarity—all so beautifully decked out in red. I share the story of my family history of breast cancer, along with the work I do to support research and awareness about this grave disease. But because breast cancer is the greatest health scare for most women, I believe heart disease is not recognized as the deadly killer it can be. As devastating as breast cancer is, I want the women in attendance to understand the very serious threat of heart disease. Even though I'm pressed for time, I don't leave early. I wind up staying until the end, and I learn a great deal from the doctor conducting the lecture. He discusses maintaining a healthy heart and preventative care.

As I leave the luncheon and head to my next appointment, I so appreciate the light of this heart-filled day. What a great day!

Thank God . . . I cannot see what lies just around the corner.

PART

1

And in the end, it's not the years in your life that count. It's the life in your years.

Abraham Lincoln

1

SWEET HOME CHICAGO

My parents both grew up in Starkville, Mississippi, and they met when they were attending Oktibbeha County Training School. My mom, Agnes Warner, was only sixteen when she and my dad, Jim Cunningham, started courting. Daddy was one grade ahead of my mother and two years older. It was not until mom was seventeen that my father was allowed to go to her house. They were allowed to sit together in the living room for two hours each evening—between 5:00 and 7:00 p.m. At 7:01 p.m. on the dot, they both knew that daddy had better be on the other side of the front door.

My mom's parents divorced when she was eight years old and when her sister, Berniece, was six. My grandmother remarried three years later. Though their biological father remained involved in their lives, their stepfather raised my mom and aunt as if they were his own children. All three parents worked long, hard hours to provide for my mom and her sister. My grandmother was a seamstress for a white family and was allowed to keep leftover fabric, which meant that my mom and her sister always had nice clothes.

Daddy graduated from high school a year before my mom. Though they weren't in school together during mom's senior year, their relationship became very serious. Mom finished high school with dreams of becoming a nurse, the same dream as her mother. But just like her mother, she was unable to attend college because she didn't have the money.

After high school, mom began babysitting for a wealthy white couple who owned the town grocery store, and daddy worked at the town's only hotel as a bellhop. One year after mom's high school graduation, daddy proposed to her. My parents were married on July 12, 1946. Their families didn't have the finances for an elaborate ceremony, so the small wedding was held at my grandparents' house—in the same room where daddy and mom had visited every evening when they were courting.

∽✖◡

When America entered World War II, men of fighting age were being drafted from all across the nation. Daddy knew that he could be drafted; and with a new wife, he was nervous. By a stroke of luck, the hotel manager's brother was the director of the draft board, and he was able to save my father from being called up. This was a huge relief. My father wasn't afraid to confront America's enemies, but sometimes he felt like less than a citizen in his own country. Fighting a war for a country that was warring against its own people didn't sit well with him.

My parents had been married for about a year when mom learned that she was pregnant with their first child. Daddy decided it was time to move up North to make a better life for his family. He announced that he was going to get them out of Starkville. My mother was stunned. She reminded my father that his employer had kept him from being drafted, and she worried that he might come after my father if he skipped town. But my father's mind was made up. He didn't want to work at a hotel for the rest of his life, and he knew he'd never be able to support a family on his bellhop wages. He decided to go to Chicago, Illinois, which was known for having a strong workforce, a variety of jobs, and great living conditions for young families.

Mom was ready to accompany him, even though she was several months pregnant. But daddy decided to go alone, figuring that he would have an easier time finding lodging and a job if he was by himself. He promised to send money home while saving as much as he could and as quickly as possible, so that my mom could join him soon thereafter. In the meantime, she moved back into her parents' home.

Even though daddy had mixed feelings about leaving his wife behind, he knew he was doing the right thing for his family and their future, and that gave him strength as he went off in pursuit of his piece of the American dream. Even with no job, no relatives or friends to greet him, no place to stay, and just a few dollars in his pocket, he was determined to make Chicago his home. A few days after he arrived, my father ran into a former neighbor from Starkville, who suggested that daddy come and stay with him until he found a place of his own. Daddy took the first job he was offered, and began his life in Chicago working at a pickle factory.

Every Monday morning, my mother received a special-delivery package with money and a letter from my dad. Though he wanted to reassure her that things were going as planned, they were honest with each other and shared their struggles and worries. Daddy's job at the pickle factory was not working out. The work was extremely hard, and the smell of the pickle juice was horrible. He knew he couldn't stay at this job much longer, and he worried that he wasn't sending enough money home to his wife. He was beginning to have doubts about whether coming to Chicago had been the correct decision.

After daddy left the pickle factory, he sought employment every day from sunrise to sunset, filling out applications wherever he saw a HELP WANTED sign. Each rejection brought great regret and guilt. The days turned into weeks, and the weeks into months.

My mother was eight months pregnant and growing impatient. But daddy encouraged her to remain with her parents until he was certain he could provide a stable home for them all. My mother reluctantly agreed. Daddy didn't share with my mother the great despair he was feeling. His hopes for their future in the North were diminishing. He labored over his decision to move to Chicago, especially when he was not with my mother on the day she delivered their first child, a girl named Marie.

Then finally, things changed. Six months after arriving in Chicago, my father was hired to pick peanuts at the E. J. Brach and Sons Candy Company. He was still living in a boardinghouse; but because he could not bear being without his wife and child any longer, he sent for them to join him. At first, the three of them lived in the boardinghouse. But after some time, my father saved enough money for them to move into a two-bedroom apartment.

In 1954, they purchased their first home on Springfield Street. The house was a duplex apartment building consisting of two flats. My parents lived on the first floor, and they rented out the second floor. A black man owning real estate was nearly unheard of at the time; but it was true. My daddy was finally beginning to live his American dream.

When word got back to family members in the South that Jim and Agnes were doing well in Chicago, our extended family began to migrate northward as well. Calls started coming in from relatives asking my parents if they could stay with them until they found a job. Without hesitation, my parents opened up their home to any family member who asked. Daddy had steady employment with E. J. Brach, and he often got other men in the family jobs there as well. My parents knew that family was supposed to help each other, and they did it for years. Even though daddy would often say it felt like people were coming out of the walls, mom always claimed that those were the happiest years of her life.

Over the next several years, my dad built a reputation for himself as a well-respected and influential man in the community. The struggles he incurred when he arrived in Chicago had stirred up a passion in him for politics, so he began volunteering as a precinct captain. The position entailed organizing and representing the community residents for the 24th Ward Democratic Party, which at the time was the strongest democratic ward in the country. Daddy represented the constituents who lived in his precinct, approximately six square blocks in the North Lawndale community on the west side of Chicago. He walked door-to-door, encouraging the residents to get out and vote; and he arranged for those who did not own vehicles to be transported to the polls. On Election Day, he volunteered at the headquarters by assisting the voters.

My dad's community service, hard work, and dedication impressed Alderman George Collins. One day he asked my father if he could do anything for him. My dad told him he could use a part-time job to help with some bills. Alderman Collins then made a call to Chicago's downtown traffic court, and subsequently daddy was hired as a part-time clerk in one of the courtrooms. It was light work with good pay and the hours were perfect, giving daddy just enough time to come home to eat dinner with his family between his two jobs.

Daddy was also making his mark at E. J. Brach. After picking peanuts for several years, he had worked his way up to foreman. While in this position, daddy witnessed unfair promotion practices. Minority workers were being hired for the lower-wage positions, but were not being promoted to any management-level positions. Daddy along with a group of his coworkers formed a coalition and raised money to retain a young lawyer, named Justin Miner, to represent them as they sought to change these unfair labor practices.

A year later, my dad was promoted to the position of assistant superintendent, where he witnessed even greater discrimination against women, blacks, and other minorities. He and the coalition continued raising the funds to keep their attorney on retainer as he gathered the information needed to file a lawsuit. After several years, Mr. Miner and my father met with the upper management of Brach and presented their charges of discrimination. Rather than allowing the case to go to trial, Brach settled out of court. Thus, new promotion practices were implemented. Qualified women and minorities were duly promoted to management positions, including my father who was promoted to senior plant superintendent. Daddy was well liked and respected, and many of his co-workers and employees considered him as the person who paved the path to success for all minorities working at Brach.

2

MIDDLE CHILD

When my parents were in their early twenties (twenty-four and twenty-six), they had their perfect family: two beautiful girls (Marie, four, and Delores, two) and a handsome baby boy, Jim Jr., who looked exactly like our father. Everyone pampered Jim Jr., constantly. Marie loved feeding her baby brother while mom worked around the house; and Delores, affectionately known as Dee, could always be found at Marie's side—watching intensely.

Nine years later and much to their surprise, my parents welcomed the arrival of twin boys: Keith and Kenneth. My father quietly awoke his nine-year-old son at 4 o'clock in the morning to tell him he had twin brothers.

Jim Jr., shocked, responded, "Twenty brothers!"

"No, twin brothers. You have *two* brothers. Now go back to sleep."

This was the beginning of the second era of the Cunningham children.

And then they had me, Daphne. I am the middle child of the second group. When I was born, Marie, Delores, and Jim Jr. (James) were in their teens, and Keith and Kenneth were three years old. Denise, my only younger sibling, was born three years after me. My mom said that she and my dad had not planned to have so many children; but as the love between them blossomed and matured, their family continued to grow.

I wasn't spoiled as a child, but I was very outspoken and curious. I was also very stubborn: If I was not allowed to share my point of view or explain my concern, I would cry and cry; or walk through the apartment huffing and puffing with my arms folded. Whenever daddy saw this behavior, he straightened me out in a hurry. Sometimes he would even allow me to plead my case after I calmed down and stopped crying. My mother didn't seem to be moved by my tears at all. As long as I wasn't hurt, she was not overly concerned.

Marie, who was sixteen years older than me, was always a mother figure to me. She was strong, mature for her age, and independent. I am told she loved to take me out in my stroller to hang with her friends. Though that didn't last long; my mother put a stop to it because she didn't want anyone to think Marie was a teen mother.

Delores and I have always been very close. She was my sister, mentor, best friend, and guiding light throughout my teen years. When my menstrual cycle began at the age of twelve, Delores was the one who taught me how to use a tampon. She was also the one who took me to the gynecologist for my first Pap smear. I had always suffered from terrible cramps, so the doctor prescribed birth control pills. Delores was also the one to explain the danger of the pill to me, warning me not to tell any boys about it because they would try to talk me into having sex. Throughout my life, so many of my lessons about life and love came from Dee.

James used me as his cover. Whenever he wanted to do something or go somewhere that our parents might question, his first defense was that he was taking me with him. If his plans changed or if he took me someplace other than where he said he would, James would always bribe me to keep his secret. He was always kind to me, and he gave me anything I asked for while we were out together. On the other hand, it was Keith and Kenneth's job to terrorize me. They often scared me into entertaining them and using a hairbrush as a microphone. Looking back on it, maybe I should thank them for directing me into my career in broadcasting!

Denise and I had a tempestuous relationship for most of our adult lives. We were as different as night and day. Denise was a very quiet child, and I was the talkative one. When we were young, we were very close and she hung on to every word I spoke. However, as we grew older, I often bullied her into doing whatever I asked of her. I shifted the treatment I received from Keith and Kenneth onto her.

✑

Although having such a big family often led to a lot of drama, we also had so many wonderful times together. The holidays were always a big deal for us, especially Christmas. My first memory of Christmas is from when I was five years old:

My mom tucked me into bed on Christmas Eve.

"Mama, do you think I'll get my Betty Brite doll tomorrow?"

"You've been a good girl, so I think you will. But you have to go to sleep before Santa comes."

Mama kissed me, went to Denise's crib and kissed her; then she left our room, closing the door behind her. I tossed and turned with sheer excitement, squeezing my eyes shut to try to force myself to sleep.

The next morning, I ran into the living room where my older brothers, Keith and Kenneth, were already playing with their cap guns and holsters as their train set ran around its small track. I looked around the room, frantically hoping that Santa had honored my request. And then I saw her—my Betty Brite doll, sitting in a high chair. I ran over and grabbed her from her seat. I couldn't believe I was finally holding her in my arms!

Delores, who was home from college for the holiday, began preparing breakfast. James was outside shoveling snow, clearing the path for friends and family who would be stopping by throughout the day. The smell of turkey, cornbread stuffing, and sweet potato pie floated through our small three-bedroom apartment. My mother was cutting out the dough for her famous dinner rolls as we all sat down for breakfast. I pulled Betty Brite's high chair to the table next to me.

"Get her out of the way!" Keith yelled. "There's no room for a stupid doll at the table!"

"There's no room for your stupid gun and police hat either!" I screamed back.

Just as I pulled my doll's chair closer to me, Keith picked up his cap gun and fired it at her.

"Ma, tell Keith to stop! He's trying to kill my doll!"

With one word, daddy brought peace to the kitchen: "Stop!"

We all shut up immediately and began eating our breakfast.

My father was a great provider, but he was not an emotional man toward his children. He did not hug us, kiss us, or pick us up in his arms. His lack of affection was normal to me. His way was simple: he made a decision or pronouncement, and his children were to obey with no questions asked. He was never hurtful or abusive; but when daddy told you to do something, you did it to the best of your ability. He brought out the strength in all of us. He made us feel like anything less than our best was a major disappointment, both to ourselves and to him. On the other hand, my mother was warm, gentle, and loving—the complete opposite of my father's tough love. She was a stay-at-home mom because my parents believed that if you make the babies, you raise the babies. My mom didn't take a part-time job until I was nine years old. By that time, Marie was twenty-five years old.

Our parents never argued in front of us. When things got heated, they went upstairs to their bedroom to deal with their issues. Growing up, I thought every household was like ours, with a hard-working father and a caring mother who took care of the home and the family. We always had everything we needed and some of what we wanted, even though there were times when it had to be put on layaway. Each night, daddy would leave our lunch money out. If we were going on a school field trip, we always had extra cash and a new outfit to wear. My dad worked two jobs to make certain that we had food, shelter, and clothing; and our lights, gas, and phone were never turned off.

When daddy was home, we all sat at the dinner table to eat our meals together; it was required. Every summer, we traveled to either Mississippi or St. Louis to visit relatives. However, one summer daddy piled my mom, my grandmother (my mother's mom), and all seven of his children into our white station wagon and took us all to Niagara Falls. That summer I was seven and Denise was four, and the two of us held each other's hands tightly as we toured the sights. That vacation is one the fondest memories I have of our family.

A PICTORIAL JOURNAL

My Journey Begins

ABOVE My dad and mom on their wedding day.

LEFT Mom reunites with my father at the boarding house shortly after arriving in Chicago for the very first time.

RIGHT It was my dad's dream to become a musician and travel with his brother. But after starting his family, his dreams changed.

LEFT Marie and Delores at ages 4 and 2.

ABOVE Marie, James, and Delores in their teen years.

ABOVE Delores' college graduation.

ABOVE Marie and my nephew, Rodney Jr.

LEFT Keith, Kenneth, Denise and me on Christmas Day.

RIGHT I'm holding my Betty Brite doll!

LEFT Dad's early years at E.J. Brach Candy Company.

ABOVE One of mom's most favorite moments, surrounded by family. That's me with my hand over my mouth, and mom probably telling me to stop talking so we can take the photo.

ABOVE I always have much to say, even on a toy phone during pre-school.

ABOVE Our family trip to Niagara Falls, Canada. So much fun.

ABOVE Keith, Denise, me, and Kenneth with Delores after her wedding.

LEFT The days when Denise and I were friends.

RIGHT Mom and dad are so cute. They enjoy each other. After seven children, they're still holding hands.

LEFT Anika and her mom, Delores.

RIGHT My college days.

ABOVE At home again, after Steve.

ABOVE It's been a long day!

ABOVE Delores poses while chaperoning the senior prom at Dunbar High School in Chicago. She loves the camera.

3

MOVING ON UP

The year I turned eight, my parents decided to rent out our first-floor unit and have a brand new house built on the south side of Chicago. Every Saturday we would pile into our Chevy Impala and go watch the builders completing our new home. My parents were so proud! A four-bedroom, three-bathroom home was quite an accomplishment for a man who came to Chicago on the train with just a few dollars in his pocket.

By the time we moved into our new home, my three older siblings were adults. Marie was married with her first child, Rodney Jr., who was only six years younger than me. Rodney was born with cerebral palsy. My mom told me he was special, but at that age I didn't understand why I couldn't play with him. One of the few times I saw my father display patience was with Rodney Jr. He was his heart.

In the new house, Keith and Kenneth shared a room, Denise and I shared a room, Delores—who was finishing college and planning her wedding—had her own room, and my parents occupied the fourth bedroom. James was working and in school then, but he would return home from time to time. Once everyone's lives settled and Delores moved out, Denise and I became the first ones in our family to have our own bedrooms. My mom thought it was a good thing that we could finally have our own space, and I think she was more excited than we were when she helped Denise and me pick out our paint and carpet colors.

When Denise and I got our own rooms, the closeness we once shared suffered greatly. We stopped having secret conversations as we lay in bed together. No longer did we share our thoughts, our feelings, and our private girl stuff. We began to argue all the time. Though all sisters have their disagreements, Denise and I were worse than most; and the little things that we should have gotten over, we never did. Our stubbornness and inability to let go of things meant that petty grievances wound up affecting our relationship for life. As teenagers, we started a pattern of pride, holding grudges, and one-upping each other that neither of us ever admitted to. As the years went on, we grew further and further apart.

Denise wasn't the only one I had a strained relationship with at that time. Keith and Kenneth were still terrorizing me at every opportunity. They started calling me "head" because they said my head was so big I looked like I was from Mars, which really affected my self-esteem. They didn't stop until mom threatened to punish them. My tears didn't move them at all; they enjoyed it when I cried. And I couldn't hurt *their* feelings no matter how I tried—and I tried very hard.

I spent many hours in my room with the door closed, listening to music or reading. It bugged my dad that I spent so much time alone in my room. Sometimes he would call me down to the basement—where he would be watching television while sitting in his recliner—just so I could scratch his head. I didn't mind it so much; daddy had soft, wavy hair. I even brushed it sometimes. I would stand behind him for a half hour or so, combing his hair, and we wouldn't say a word to each other. He'd watch television; I'd brush his hair.

Delores always came over on Saturdays to spend time with mom. Sometimes they'd go out shopping, but mostly they'd just sit in the kitchen and talk for hours. Delores majored in English in college, and she was on us constantly about our speech and pronunciation. "Do you know how important it is for you to speak correctly?" she'd lecture. "You weren't raised on the streets, and you are not going to speak like you were."

~

Daddy was very strict, especially with his girls. We weren't allowed to receive phone calls from boys until we were fifteen, and we couldn't date until we turned sixteen. If a boy wanted to get on my father's bad side, all he had to do was show up at our house with his shoes unlaced. To my father, that was an undeniable sign that the boy was lazy.

"If a young man can't bend down to tie his shoes, he won't walk in them long enough to make something of himself," my dad said, and he stood by it.

My father, whose old-fashioned values bordered on chauvinism, did not hold my brothers to the same rules as the girls, whether for dating, curfews, or chores. At one point, mom decided to divide the household chores among Denise, Keith, Kenneth, and me. We rotated each week. This was the perfect arrangement—until one day, daddy came home and saw Keith at the sink washing dishes.

"What are you doing?" daddy asked angrily.

"It's my week to do the dishes," Keith replied.

Daddy shut that down immediately. He said that it was not a boy's place to wash dishes; it was the girls' responsibility. And so, despite my mom's efforts, he reassigned our chores. The boys would mop and vacuum the floors, clean the toilets, take out the trash, and mow the lawn. All the other inside work belonged to Denise and me. I was upset and disappointed, and I cried so hard I got a headache. I didn't speak to my dad for days after that.

To this day I believe he made the wrong choice. I think all boys should learn how to do laundry, wash dishes, and do other "women's work," because it will ultimately make them better men and better husbands. But I now know that even as an adult, my father was called "boy" by white men, and it was crucially important to him that his sons never felt domesticated or spoken down to, and that they always had the "manly" role in the household.

On Saturdays, we all had to clean the house from top to bottom before even considering going out with friends. Daddy didn't just assume we'd done what we were supposed to do; he checked behind us to make sure. I once overheard my mom telling him that his kids were not his employees, and that he acted more like a drill sergeant than a father. My dad responded passionately and indicated that he was trying to teach us responsibility and discipline. He wanted his children to know that there were no shortcuts in life.

I really disliked my dad while I was growing up, and I believed he disliked me too. But I could always count on mom to keep the mood light. She loved Al Green and Marvin Gaye, and she always played music while we were doing chores. She would hum along as she cleaned and sometimes the music would move her down to the basement, where it was not unusual to see our parents share a dance. I loved to sneak down the steps to watch them. Dad was so smooth as he and my mom swayed together or did the two-step. Seeing that always made me smile.

❧

Mom and dad wouldn't let me go to the neighborhood high school, Fenger, because they felt there were too many students per class and worried I'd get lost in the crowd. By this time, Delores was a teacher at Dunbar High School and she suggested I attend school there, which I decided to do. It was an inner-city school. And my parents wouldn't allow me to take public transportation that far. So every night my mom would drop me off at Delores' house, and I'd commute to school with her.

I loved Delores, but being a teacher's sister did not make me very popular. The teachers held me to a higher standard than the other students. If I was in the hall after the bell rang, I would hear, "Daphne, you should know better! You are a teacher's sister; you ought to be setting a better example." If I cut class, Delores was the first to hear about it, and she'd come down hard on me on our ride home.

I began to regret my decision to go to Dunbar high school, and I told my parents I wanted to transfer. Of course my dad would not hear of it. He had explained to me, before I committed to my decision, the possible challenges I would face. He had encouraged me to think long and hard about my choice, and would not let me go back on it now. Though I believed he was being too strict and completely unfair, I did eventually find my place at Dunbar.

To be honest, I was not a great student. I had to study long and hard to earn Bs and sometimes Cs. My teachers often told my parents that if I didn't talk so much during class, I'd be a much better student. My dad was always great at math; but unfortunately, I did not inherit this skill. He would check our homework every night, making any corrections on a separate piece of paper from which I would copy before school the next day. My achievements in math were all because of his help.

My father was also musically talented. He played the saxophone, and his brother played both the saxophone and the clarinet. When my uncle died, he left his clarinet to my dad. And when I was a sophomore in high school, my dad decided I would learn to play it to honor his brother's memory. The only problem was that I wanted to play the piano. Even though I was old enough to make my own decision, I desperately sought my dad's approval. I thought that my playing the clarinet would give him a reason to like me. Well, I took lessons and daddy supported me; but he never complimented me—not once. During performances, I would look out into the audience and see him; but once the concert was over, he never acknowledged my performance. This was the beginning of my learned behavior: to please others before attempting to please myself. I spent so much of my life trying to win my father's heart and acceptance that I eventually lost track of the woman I wanted to be.

I never questioned whether my dad loved me. But the lack of hugs and kisses as a girl affected me as a woman. My father didn't refuse his affection because he chose to, but because he didn't know how to show how he felt. I didn't know I needed affection from my daddy; I never had it. So I never knew it was missing. However, I've learned that you *can* miss what you never had. Now that I am an adult, sometimes I still feel as if I'm looking for a hug from my daddy. Our level of emotional stability as girls, I believe, will determine both the women we become and the type of men we choose.

4

Hot Fun in the Summertime

I love the summer. Not only is my birthday in the summer, but also school is out. However, summer vacation did not mean we could take it easy. Once you turned sixteen in our house, you worked, volunteered in the community, or went to summer school. I didn't mind working during the summer. I learned to type during my sophomore year, so I was always able to find a part-time job at a bank or a business office.

The summer before I began my junior year, Delores and her husband, Fred, managed a camp called Pleasant Valley in Woodstock, Illinois, about two hours from Chicago. After my job ended, my parents gave me permission to spend the last two weeks of my summer vacation there. Even though it wasn't far from Chicago, it felt like another world to me. Pleasant Valley was a huge farm. Delores and her family lived on the top of a hill in a yellow house. The staff and visitors stayed in dorm-like rooms about fifty yards away from them. That summer, Delores allowed me to stay in one of the dorms. I loved it; I felt so grown up. We went swimming during the day, rode on hayrides in the evening, roasted marshmallows and lay beneath the stars for hours. Delores and Fred allowed me to roam free around the grounds. Every now and then, I would run up the hill to the house to sit and chat with Delores and to play with her daughter, Lisa, for a while— before heading back to the pool or hanging out with the staff.

Both Delores and Fred were schoolteachers, and that summer, one of Fred's students, Joe, worked at Pleasant Valley. I first met Joe when I was fourteen because Fred often planned weekend trips with his students and would take Keith, Kenneth, and me along. Joe was seventeen and I was sixteen. I liked him—*a lot*. One day, Joe was giving me swimming lessons and he kissed me on the lips. I was pleasantly surprised, and I kissed him back. We kissed that day until our lips were chapped. Eventually, Joe went back to work; but he asked me to meet him at his cabin later.

I knew I could talk to Delores about anything; I could share with her all the things I didn't feel comfortable sharing with my mom. And Delores didn't hold back when I asked her questions about boys and sex. After Joe left that afternoon, I ran up the hill to Dee's house. I told her that I liked Joe, and I thought he liked me too. With forced casualness, I mentioned that he asked me to meet him at his cabin that night, and that I thought he wanted to have sex with me. Delores sat next to me. I listened as she calmly but firmly explained why I should wait, and what it would mean if I didn't. She was absolutely right, and I knew it.

When I met Joe at his cabin later, I told him I couldn't have sex with him. He explained that he did not want to have sex, because he knew he'd get fired if we did. I'm sure he was lying because I embarrassed him, but we had a good time together anyway. I left Pleasant Valley the same way I had arrived: a virgin.

My mother didn't think all the girls I hung out with were suited for me; a couple of them were a few years older and much more mature. She worried that they would cause me to grow up too fast. One of my friends, Veronica, fell into that category. Kenneth and Veronica were dating, but she and I were friends too. I looked up to Veronica and could be easily influenced by her. Right before school started that summer, Keith, Kenneth, and I were hanging out in the basement one night with a handful of our friends. I was talking to my friend, Allison, when Veronica suggested that the three of us go outside. It was a warm clear night as we headed toward my backyard and stopped beneath my bedroom window. I always kept my bedroom window open, and as I looked up, I saw my curtains blowing from the night breeze. My parents' bedroom was across from mine, but located in the back of the house overlooking the backyard.

When Veronica told us she had some weed, I was scared. I didn't want to smoke it. She assured me that I could just get a "contact high" from her blowing smoke in my face. So the three of us waited as Veronica lit the joint. She took the first puff and held it in for a few seconds, then blew it into Allison's nose. Allison began coughing and laughing at the same time. Veronica took another puff and came toward me. I closed my eyes and stood as stiff as a board while she cupped her hands and blew the smoke into my nostrils. It burned like crazy.

Seconds later we were all laughing. We stood outside awhile longer, and then Veronica pulled a bottle of "smell good" from her purse. After we doused ourselves with the perfume, we walked into the house as if we were very cool.

There was a bathroom near the kitchen; and as the three of us were heading there, the phone rang. From where I stood talking on the phone, I could see up the stairs. Suddenly, my mom walked out of my bedroom. I nearly fainted—Mama had been in my room while we were outside getting high! She didn't say a word; she just stood at the top of the stairs looking at me.

I couldn't form any words; my mind was confused and blank. As my mouth hung open, my mother calmly reminded me that I had someone on the phone. Then she turned and walked into her bedroom, shutting the door behind her. I hung up the phone and ran to the bathroom to tell Veronica and Allison what happened. They made haste getting out of the house. Then I called Keith and Kenneth upstairs and told them that the party was over "now!"

"What did you do Daphne? You look high!" Kenneth shouted.

"You smoking reefer, Daphne? Are you stupid?" Keith asked as he leaned into my face. "Who gave you reefer?"

"Veronica did." I responded.

"Veronica? She must be trippin," Kenneth snapped.

They chastised me for acting like a fool, and said that if Mama found out, we would never be allowed to have another party.

"Mama knows," I said, crying.

"How does Mama know?" Kenneth asked angrily.

"'Cause she was in my room, and we were in the driveway under my bedroom window!"

"Girl, daddy is going to kill you," Keith said.

I stood sobbing as Keith and Kenneth emptied the basement. After everyone left, they ripped into me for several minutes more. They called me stupid. And reminded me again and again that if we couldn't have any more parties, I was going to pay. Then Keith eased into my room and grabbed something for me to change into, and Kenneth threw my weed-smelling clothes in the washer. He even took air freshener outside and sprayed it up and down the driveway. I was a nervous wreck as I headed to my room, and I didn't sleep the entire night. The next morning, I was afraid to come out of my room. Keith and Kenneth came in and told me I couldn't hide forever. I knew that, but my mother's silence was driving me crazy. Mama finally knocked on my door. When she came in, she sat on my bed and told me how badly I had hurt her.

"I never say what my kids will or won't do. But I had no idea you did drugs, Daphne," Mama said sadly.

"I *don't* do drugs, Mama, I promise! That was the first time." I gulped, and then asked, "Are you going to tell daddy?"

"You damn kids; the things I can't tell your father."

"Mama, I'm sorry!"

"Sorry? You have a drug problem, Daphne. Now I have to find a place to get you cleaned up."

My mom was serious about sending me to rehab, but my older brother James assured her that I didn't need to go, even though he couldn't convince her the drug wasn't dangerous. I didn't get off easily though: I couldn't go out after school, have company on the weekends, or use the telephone for weeks. When I did start going out again, my mom checked on me rigorously. As soon as I walked in the door—even if I was coming in from church—she called me to her, looked deep into my eyes, and then smelled my breath and my clothes. This went on for months. But she never did mention it to daddy.

PART

2

5

If I'd Only Known Then...

*I*t wasn't until my freshman year of college that I began to understand my father as a man, and not just as the head of our household. Being out of the house gave me the opportunity to reflect on our relationship. I thought about his strong discipline and direct tactics. Now I was finally able to do whatever I wanted, without his being there to tell me "no." I did my share of mischief in college, but I began to mature after I left home. I felt responsible for the first time. Being away from home was good for me. I still wasn't the best student, but I surrounded myself with smart people who helped me form good study habits.

I continued to date my high school sweetheart, my first love whom I'll call Steve. No one in my family was happy with my dating him, especially once I'd left home. Everyone thought Steve was a nice young man; they just didn't think he was right for me. It angered my mom that Steve was visiting me every other weekend. Daddy told me I was compromising and settling; that

Steve lacked ambition. Delores had hoped I would meet new young men in college, and not be in such a serious relationship at my age. She told me how disappointed she was in me, and what a bad decision I was making by remaining in that relationship.

Of course, I didn't listen. I was eighteen, on my own, and felt like they had no right to tell me what to do. But even I knew I was outgrowing the relationship. Although my desire for Steve was fading, I stayed with him. He was familiar and comfortable. I knew in my heart that these were the wrong reasons to remain in a relationship. I also knew we were too young to be exclusive. But I spent my entire childhood trying to please my father, and feeling no affection from him. I was desperate for love and validation, which Steve provided for me. He complimented me, he was attentive, he knew when to hug me, and most of the time he was kind to me. I convinced myself that was enough.

ᜒᜐᜐ

After college, Steve and I were still together. I was working full-time as a customer service agent with a major airline; Steve was also working full-time. Getting married and having a family weren't my top priorities. I was more driven by the thoughts of having a successful career.

Steve and I were both raised in church, but I was Methodist and he was Baptist. He later joined a church that was part of the Apostolic faith. I knew nothing about this religion, but I began attending services with him. They were quite different from the ones I was used to. However the people were warm and caring, and the love I felt there was so strong. How they worshipped, how they prayed, and how the pastor ministered the Word was mind-blowing.

I was fine with everything until I was asked if I wanted to be saved. "Saved? What's that?" I asked. As one of the women attempted to explain the apostolic plan of salvation to me, I withdrew a bit—though no one tried to force me to make a decision. Nevertheless I continued to attend the church, and I grew in faith. I became more God-conscious and intrigued with the lifestyle of the people within the congregation. I never made any plans to join the church or to be saved, but things started to change for me.

One New Year's Eve, Steve and I attended a service at the church, where the pastor spoke about the love of Christ. I was amazed at this beautiful celebration that brought God in with the beginning of a new year filled with promises and reconciliation. A couple of minutes before midnight, the pastor stopped the service and led the congregation in prayer to usher in the new year. His words were powerful, full of blessings, hope, and the new beginnings that filled the hearts of those with bowed heads, humbled in the presence of the Lord. After he ended the prayer, he asked if anyone wanted to give his or her life to Christ. Without hesitation and without thinking about it, I got up from my seat and headed down the aisle to accept his invitation. I asked God to forgive me of all my sins and to give me a heart toward him. That was it. I wasn't nervous about it. It felt right. I received the greatest gift of my life that night: a relationship with Christ.

After that, I became a part of my new church family. Steve and I developed relationships with those in our age group, but we were the only unmarried couple. Thus, people began to push us toward marriage. I was still unsure about my future. I couldn't understand why it seemed like I was being forced to do something I wasn't ready to do. So I met with my pastor. I asked him why it was such a big deal to everyone that we marry, and he explained his biblical views on the rights of marriage. He shared chapter 7 in the book of 1Corinthians. His focus was on verse 9: "It is better to marry than to burn." My pastor explained that *burn* meant to burn with lust. While I understood where he was coming from, I didn't agree with that being reason enough to get married.

My pastor was clear, assuring me that indeed it was not reason enough to marry. But, Steve and I became more and more influenced by our environment. We began to succumb to the pressure. Before long, we were making wedding plans. I didn't know a lot about the Bible during this time, but I knew I wanted to be doing what was right. As usual, I considered everyone but Daphne as I made plans to do something that would change my whole life—just because everyone else thought it was the proper thing to do.

I knew Steve was not my true-life partner; but against my better judgment, I decided to marry him. My family tried to stop me. My mom even pleaded with me to wait at least a year. She felt that if she could get me to postpone our nuptials, she was sure I would change my mind. She believed my head was clouded with promises, and given enough time, the future would reveal that Steve could not keep them. My dad also told me how disappointed he was with my decision. Over and over he told me that I was too young, that I hadn't even begun to live yet, and that I was making one of the biggest mistakes of my life. Still I refused to listen. As a result of my family's constant pressure to end my engagement, I completely shut them out. But despite their conviction that I was making a terrible mistake, my parents still stood by me.

On my wedding day, as my dad and I were waiting to walk down the aisle, he looked into my eyes and said, "It's not too late. You can stop this ceremony right now and I'll take you home."

"No, daddy," I said stubbornly. "Let's go."

The doors opened, and I cried all the way down the aisle. I wanted to turn and run, but my feet kept moving forward. I share this story as a warning: If you are questioning any decision in your life or if you are the least bit unsure or uncomfortable about your choice, please pause until you are sure you are doing the right thing for *you*. I believe we all know in our hearts when something or someone is right or wrong for us; this is our "personal truth." Know yourself and know what is best for you! Love yourself first based on what is truly in your heart. If only I had heeded my own advice!

Needless to say, my marriage to Steve was a disaster. It wasn't long before I knew for sure that I'd made a huge mistake. But my pride wouldn't allow me to go to my parents and admit they were right. I was too ashamed even to go to Delores for advice. Instead, I kept my mouth shut and kept a smile painted on my face whenever I went to church, to work, or to see my family and friends.

My lack of self-esteem and my desire to please those around me were major forces in my life at that time. I took myself out of the equation and did what I felt was expected of me. This should have been all the proof I needed to realize I wasn't mature enough to be someone's wife. I shouldn't even have been a girlfriend at that point! I didn't know or understand myself as an individual. How could I be good for anyone if I could not be good for myself?

In my marriage to Steve, there were many struggles: financial, spiritual, physical, and emotional. I was so uninvolved in my own life that I hadn't asked Steve any important questions before we got married. We'd never discussed our finances, our goals, our career choices, or whether we wanted to have children. We hadn't even talked about where we planned to live. Looking back on it all now, we were merely playing house—except it wasn't a game. That relationship broke me down. I became less of a woman and lost more of myself. I lived in the shadows of happiness and peace. And eventually, I became a victim of domestic violence.

I have forgotten most of the abusive moments, but I remember the first one. I was questioning Steve about spending the night away from home without an explanation. He became extremely angry and grabbed my hair, pulled me across the apartment to the front door, and shoved me out into the hall. I didn't have the keys to my car, so I took the elevator down to the lobby and walked to the park near our apartment building where I watched Steve drive away. When he left, I headed back to the apartment; and the maintenance man unlocked our door. I packed a bag, called a friend from church, and spent the next two nights with her family.

I had known Steve since I was thirteen years old. He never displayed violent behavior toward me in the past; but once he did it the first time, it kept happening. Ladies: If a man ever strikes you, grabs you, or shoves you, get away from him *immediately*. It doesn't matter how sorry he says he is; it doesn't matter if he tells you it will never happen again. Until he receives some form of counseling and anger management, he is unfit to be with you.

By that time, Steve was the choir director. I didn't want anyone to think differently of him; so to protect his image (and my own), I hid the abuse from our family, friends, co-workers, and church members. I cared more about people's perception of our family than I did about myself. In public, Steve was always caring, warm, and compassionate; he seemed like the model husband. But behind closed doors, his rage was becoming uncontrollable. In addition, we were always in trouble financially. Steve was offered many employment opportunities, but his lack of motivation and responsibility made it impossible for him to keep a job. And eventually people stopped extending helping hands.

Finally, I reached the point where I couldn't take it anymore and so I went to my pastor to seek guidance. It was during that meeting when I realized I had blamed myself for the physical abuse, the emotional neglect, and the lack of financial support. I saw clearly, for the first time, that here was another man I was trying to please and another man whom I wanted to like me at any cost. As I sat there, it hit me like a ton of bricks: my father was the first man in my life, and he created the model I had for my relationships with men. I always tried so hard to please him, but I never got the affection I needed in return.

My pastor, a kind, softhearted, emotionally available man, became a fatherly figure in my life. He cared for his congregation and had no problem expressing it. I watched how he behaved with his wife and children. His tender heart touched me greatly. I grew very fond of him. He showed me a new model for the kind of relationships I could have.

After I'd shared my marriage troubles with him, he asked me what I wanted to do. I responded by saying, as I always did, that I wanted to do what was right. But this time it was different: I wanted to do what was right for *me*. Finally it was about me: what I wanted, what I needed, how I felt, and what I deserved. For the first time in my life, I felt I deserved more.

As my pastor and I talked, I felt the weight lift from my shoulders. I became freer in my mind and spirit than I had been in years. As our conservation came to a close, my pastor said very softly, "I am sorry I didn't advise you better before you married." That meant more to me than he could have known. He was the first man to ever apologize to me.

I was terrified about swallowing my pride and telling my parents about everything, and I waited for more than a month before doing so. However when I sat them down to tell them there was no "I told you so," there was no lecture given, and there was no judgment cast upon me. When I finished, my father merely said, "If you need to come home, you can." He touched my shoulder and then left the room.

Mom and I continued to talk. When I told her that I had been physically abused, I was quick to explain that it wasn't all Steve's fault and that I was wrong too. She asked me three questions:

"Did you ever see your father hit me?"

"No, ma'am."

"Did you ever see your father raise his hand to me?"

"No, ma'am."

"Then what made it okay for Steve to beat *your* ass?"

I didn't have an answer for her. I knew I'd accepted some things that I shouldn't have because of my lack of self-esteem and my inability to distinguish between genuine love and seeking love. I took the abuse because I didn't know I deserved better. I didn't know if this was an acceptable way for a man to show his love because I had never been properly taught what love was. In fact, it wasn't until my father laid his hands on my shoulder that day and told me I could come home that I ever *felt* his love.

6

STARTING OVER

Someone once told me, "Life is full of tests. Don't get too comfortable once you've excelled at a learning experience because there's another one right behind, waiting to tap you on the shoulder." Sometimes, if you are fortunate, you get to rest between the tests—but never for long. Life experiences are designed to challenge us. After completing each challenge, you should gain clarity, knowledge, and purpose. Some events are meant to build us up as individuals, and others are meant to take us to the next level in our lives and make us strong. These are the tests that prove your true character.

I was slowly moving on with my life after my failed marriage. Even though I had a long way to go, I was building my self-esteem and learning to like and accept myself as an individual. That's when I felt a tap on my shoulder: my Aunt Berniece, mom's only sister, was diagnosed with colon cancer. I didn't learn of my aunt's illness until it was in its final stages. While the prognosis was not great, my aunt had hope. I was not very close to her, but of course I loved her, and I visited her whenever I could.

My aunt wasn't very spiritual, but one day I saw a book by Oral Roberts on her bedside table. This gave me an opportunity to talk with her about healing. (Isn't it amazing how the universe lines up opportunities for us?) That conversation led to a new relationship between the two of us. She began sharing her most intimate thoughts with me. We talked freely about her disease and how she turned to the Bible and spiritual readings as a source of encouragement.

From that point forward, I shared the scripture with her and sought out books and music for her to use in her daily meditation. I wanted her to be able to leave this world with peace and comfort. I wanted her to know there was life after death. I wanted her to know we all loved her, but God loved her more than any of us ever could. I wanted her to know she could see God's face in peace.

We met at least once a week to pray and study together, and she began to develop a strong relationship with Christ. The transition was remarkable, and it was beautiful to watch. Even though she continued to grow weaker physically, spiritually she was soaring. We even talked about life after death. She wasn't holding on to this physical world as strongly; she was embracing something greater.

When she reached a place in her treatment where she felt physically able, she decided to attend church with me. Her faith had reached a new milestone, and spiritually she was so strong! One evening as we were driving to church, she turned off the music as we sat at a red light. She looked at me and said, "Who would have ever thought you would be the one to rescue me?"

I didn't view it as rescuing her; I saw it as doing what I knew needed to be done. "I love you, Aunt Niecy," I said with deep compassion.

"I love you too, Daphne."

That was the first and last time my aunt told me she loved me.

As my aunt grew closer to death, it was not easy for me to comfort my mom. I had to let her find her own acceptance. But my dad stayed so close to her, I wondered if she could breathe. I knew the love they shared would give my mom the strength she needed.

My Aunt Niecy passed away the following summer. She was fifty-six years old. As we stood at the burial site, it gave me great comfort to know that only the shell of her was going into the ground and not her spirit. She is in a better place. She'd made her peace with Christ and was received back to Him. I feel so blessed that I was able to share the last few months of her life with her.

It took about a year after my marriage ended for me to start feeling balance, peace, and self-assurance. I was still living with my parents, and my dad and I began to bond for the first time. He and I spent more time together and talked about politics and world events. Even though he still didn't hug or kiss me, we were definitely becoming closer.

I was working for an airline, a position I'd only taken as a temporary assignment, but it turned out to be a wonderful job. I began to do a lot of traveling. I took weekend trips to New York, and traveled abroad as often as I could. I was able to get discounts on airfare for my family as well, and when my parents went to Europe for the first time, they made me feel like I had given them the best gift ever. It was incredible to hear them share their experiences as they toured the vacation spots of their choice. I stayed with the airline for a while and took some classes during the evenings to continue my studies.

Though it took many years, Steve and I are on good terms now. We have a cordial relationship, and there is no more anger or bitterness between us. We have both grown, and all is forgiven. Looking back on it now, it's easy to see that we were just too young and too immature to be in an adult relationship.

My newfound self-love made it possible for me to become more open to receiving positive things into my life, and my spirituality was stronger than ever after the passing of Aunt Niecy. I continued to regularly attend church service and sing in the choir.

Our church's Sunday services were recorded to air on the radio. One Sunday, our minister of music asked if I would consider announcing the radio broadcast services. I wasn't sure if I'd be able to do it in front of all those people, but he encouraged me to think about it. After much prompting from my friends, I agreed to give it a try.

From then on, every Sunday morning I would sit in the pulpit and introduce our pastor. Before the service ended, I would go upstairs to our sound room and record the radio tag for the broadcast that would air the following Friday. This was the beginning of my broadcasting career. I enjoyed being behind the microphone. I felt at home in that space.

7

THEN CAME YOU

ne summer day, word spread throughout the
church that the football player Todd Bell had
begun attending our services. I didn't know
much about him; only that he played football with the Chicago
Bears. Though plenty of other women paid him a lot of attention!

I was in the pulpit preparing to introduce the pastor one
Sunday when I caught Todd staring at me. I admit I was flattered
to have his attention; but as he continued to stare, he actually
made me feel a bit uncomfortable. I did think he was handsome
though. He was caramel-colored and tall, with a toned body, broad
shoulders, a slender waist, and a really nice behind.

Later that afternoon, Todd approached me and asked my
name. We chatted for a few minutes, and then he asked for my
phone number. I respectfully declined. I was still reeling from
my failed marriage, and though I was very attracted to Todd, I
wouldn't allow myself to let my guard down. I didn't believe I
was ready to even start thinking about another relationship. Many

years later, Todd told me that as a football player he knew he could have almost any woman he wanted. And it was my lack of interest that had attracted him to me back then.

After a full year of cordial hellos and goodbyes, the ice was finally broken between us. One Sunday, after I finished the close of our service, I headed downstairs to go home. The church was empty, but waiting in the front lobby was Todd. Our eyes met, and he told me he had been wondering for months where I disappeared to before church ended. We engaged in some idle chitchat, and then Todd asked me for my number again. This time I was ready to give it to him. He called me the same evening and we talked for six straight hours. That was the beginning of our friendship.

Todd captured my heart without any physical contact in the beginning stages of our relationship. We took a long time to get to know one another. He made me laugh, even though he was a very intense man. Our conversations about family and goals revealed great similarities between us. However, the first time I told him about my marriage, he was stunned. Todd was a very religious man, and he frowned on divorce. He wanted to know everything, and I didn't lie to him. I went on to explain that if my failed marriage were a problem for him, it would be fine. It was in my past and I couldn't change that; but I completely understood his concern.

We didn't talk for several weeks after that. When he did call, he asked if we could move forward slowly with our relationship. I was hesitant. After the hell I'd experienced in my marriage, I'd made up my mind that I didn't want anything or anyone whom God didn't want for me. I was not going to force any relationship to fit into my life again. But Todd and I talked it out, and we came to an understanding.

We didn't go out on dates. We maintained our telephone-only relationship during that entire football season. At the end of the year, Todd returned to Columbus, Ohio, to finish his degree at Ohio State University. I didn't speak to him for nearly half a year, but he phoned the following May when he arrived in Chicago for the Bears' training camp. Our conversation was just as fulfilling as it had always been.

Over the next several years, Todd and I experienced many twists and turns. Though we were always friends, we were a roller coaster of on-again and off-again, as far as a romance went. The relationship was not serious for either of us, but we learned a lot about each other and continued to grow closer.

I already knew Todd was a great athlete. In fact, he was what is known as a Blue Chip All-American. When he finished high school, he received a great deal of attention from coaches, and he could go to any university of his choice. After considering all of his options, he decided to attend the University of Southern California. Then one day, Woody Hayes, the head football coach of Ohio State University (OSU), showed up at his parents' house. Todd hadn't even considered OSU because he was from Ohio and was desperate to get out of the Buckeye State. But Coach Hayes spent the entire day with Todd, and managed to change his mind. Todd gained so much more than a starting position with the Buckeyes. He once told me that his relationship with Coach Woody changed his life. Woody Hayes was more than a coach; he was Todd's mentor, teacher, and friend.

Todd was drafted by the Chicago Bears during his junior year at Ohio State University, and subsequently played with them for nearly his entire football career. In the third year of our relationship, Todd invited me to come to some of the home games at the Chicago Bears Stadium and to sit with the other players' friends and families. I agreed to come, even though I didn't know a thing about football. I thought the game was boring, the fans were crazy, and the noise level was ridiculous. "And people say church folks are loud!" I'd say to myself as I watched the sea of people in blue and orange scream and shout for their beloved Bears. But Todd was so passionate about football, and over time, his attentive nature led him to take the time to explain the game to me. I actually grew to love the sport. Plus, I certainly enjoyed watching him! When he was on the field, he was *fierce*: aggressive and compassionate at the same time. He would knock the wind out of someone, and then extend his hand to help him back to his feet.

As I attended the games more often, people started to notice. Women wanted to know who I was and whom I was with. When I would say I was a friend of Todd Bell, they would pry further by asking if I was his girlfriend or fiancée. I wanted to say "None of your business," but decided not to respond at all. The wives of the other players were generally friendly toward me, but a few of the girlfriends—and especially the wannabe girlfriends— were not as kind. Being a professional athlete's girlfriend was an adjustment, to say the least.

8

To Have and To hold

Four years after our first official meeting, Todd and I finally considered ourselves a couple. But I still had to deal with the masses of females who were attracted to him. I admit I wasn't a big fan of the attention Todd was getting. Women often disregarded me completely to get within his presence to chat, pass him their number, or ask for his autograph. I knew this came with his position—and usually I would be content to hang out in the background—but these women could be unbelievably brazen. There were times when we would be holding hands and a woman would have the nerve to walk between us, causing our hands to separate, and would then deliberately turn her back to me to address Todd. The first time that occurred, I asked Todd if he'd noticed what had happened. Not only did he say he had, but he didn't think it was a big deal! It *wasn't* a big deal; it was the principle. I knew exactly what these women were after.

Once, Todd and I were at a black-tie event when a woman introduced herself to us. She chatted with Todd for a few moments, and then walked away. Later that night, when Todd removed his jacket and handed it to me, I noticed something in the pocket. Todd didn't know what it was; but we looked closer and realized that it was the woman's photo with a phone number on the back! I had to give her credit for being so slick and for making her move directly in front of me.

Eventually I learned not to sweat the small stuff. I learned not to watch the women, but rather to keep my eyes on Todd. How *he* handled the situation is what mattered to me. I told Todd that as long as he never gave me a reason not to, I would always trust him. I kept my guard up. These other women were not going anywhere; they would always be around. I had to learn to be secure enough in our relationship so that it didn't get to me.

⁛

The holidays have always been major events for our family, and during Christmas we would go all out. The first Christmas Todd and I spent together as a couple, dinner was at my late Aunt Niecy's home where her daughter, Altricia, lived with her father and two children. Todd was very comfortable and relaxed around my family. After our meal, we headed downstairs for our gift exchange.

Todd sat on the opposite side of the room from me, quietly watching the scene. There were plenty of children running around, sharing their toys with one another. Keith's daughter, Tiffany, was born prematurely just before the holidays. At first we feared she might not survive, but her tiny body had healed. Now she was the center of everyone's attention. She was our Christmas miracle. Everyone was full and happy as we exchanged gifts. The Christmas tree was bright and the smell of pine filled the basement. We were all sitting and talking when a folded piece of paper was passed down to me. Confused, I unfolded it and read. To say I was shocked is putting it mildly—it was a marriage proposal!

He'd written it like the notes girls received from boys in grade school: "Will you marry me?" with a box for yes and a box for no.

I laughed nervously and looked over at Todd. He mouthed the words, "I'm serious." I have always been a very private person; so I tried not to show any emotion, which is a behavior I learned from my dad. Luckily, my family was so engrossed in their own conversations that no one had paid any attention to the note that they had passed my way. I hurried up the stairs to the bathroom. After I calmed myself, I called my mom to come up and showed her the note. We sat on the edge of the tub for several minutes before speaking.

My mother was fond of Todd, but she didn't know him that well. She knew I loved him; but after what I had gone through with Steve, she was understandably cautious. She asked me if I was attracted to Todd because of *who* he was or *what* he was. She asked whether he had ever displayed any abusive behavior toward me—even just raising his voice. She asked me how I felt about spending the rest of my life with him. We talked about it for a while, and I told her how nervous and excited the proposal made me. I was so surprised; I hadn't expected anything like this. She put her arms around me and told me, "This is your life and your decision." Mom and I headed back downstairs, and Todd asked me to return the note with my answer. My heart was racing and my hands were shaking as I quickly checked "yes" and handed it back to him. He smiled and tucked it into his pocket.

On the ride back to my parents' house, I asked him why he'd chosen to propose that day. He told me my family made him feel like such a part of us. And as he watched the closeness we shared, he knew he wanted a family of his own with me. My heart had never been touched like that before. I had tried not to open up my heart; however, I knew I was letting my guard down. In the hole where there was the pain of my first marriage, love was filling it up. It was difficult to turn my emotions off.

"I love you." Todd said.

It was the first time he'd said that, but his actions had already convinced me of his love.

⸎

We picked out my ring the following week, and he gave me a Mercedes Benz car as an engagement gift. He took it to my parents' home. It sat in the garage for more than a year before I would drive it. The ring stayed in the box in my closet for the same amount of time. No one other than my mother and Delores knew about our engagement. I was still nervous and guarded, and I'd made up my mind that I was not going to put our engagement on display, only to have it blow up in my face later.

Nevertheless, things were going well with Todd and me. By now we had our wedding date set and were working out the details. I did not want a large wedding; I would have been fine with just going into the pastor's office to exchange our vows. But Todd had other plans. He wanted all the bells and whistles. With a bit of reluctance, I conceded.

I asked my sisters to be my bridesmaids. Delores agreed, but Marie declined because she believed she was too old to be a bridesmaid. Denise refused also; though she didn't tell me why. My mom insisted on my urging Denise to be a bridesmaid. I asked her twice, but each time she declined. I flatly refused to beg Denise to be a part of my wedding. I never asked her why she wouldn't do it, but I think she may have been jealous. She'd always been the pretty one; the one who caused men's mouths to fall open when she walked into a room. I think she felt that if one of us married a professional athlete, it should have been her.

The wedding plans were under way, but my relationship with Todd continued to experience many peaks and valleys. Before he returned home to attend classes at Ohio State in December, he showed me a letter he'd written to himself while he was in college. The letter described the kind of wife and family he wanted one day. When I finished reading it, I told him how beautifully written it was. He said I was the woman he'd written about before he even knew me.

As we kept talking, I realized that there was more that he wanted to say; but he was having trouble spitting it out. Finally, he admitted that my previous marriage was troubling him. He felt that because he wouldn't be my first husband, it would take something away from how he envisioned his life. Four years earlier I'd told him that if my past failed marriage were a problem, I would understand. Now, all of a sudden, he didn't see me, Daphne, as the woman whom he'd fallen in love with and asked to be his wife. He wasn't sure if he wanted to carry a woman with baggage. I was furious. I had finally let my guard down; and just as I'd feared, everything was collapsing around me. I told Todd that I would not live under the umbrella of my past; nor would I let him hold it against me. He tried to explain that wasn't what he was doing.

"I just never thought I would marry a divorced woman," he said.

My feelings of hurt and devastation were immeasurable. We were four years deep by now. But just as he remembered my past, so did I. Every day! It was situations like this that did not allow me to forget. I told him again what I'd told him four years prior—I didn't want anyone or anything God didn't want for me. I was not willing to compromise my growth, not even for something most women would die for: to be the wife of a professional athlete.

Todd called off our engagement. My heart was broken; but I was so glad I hadn't worn the ring or shared my relationship with my friends and co-workers. That would have made everything so much worse! I held my head up during the day, cried myself to sleep at night, and prepared to move on.

❧

At the end of January, Todd decided to visit his family in Middletown, Ohio. While there, he spent some time with an elderly gentleman whom he greatly respected. They talked about the future and Todd asked him for advice. Todd talked about me and explained his issues with my first marriage. His friend asked him a series of questions about how I treated him, his feelings for me, and so on. He reminded Todd that no one gets it all because no one is perfect, and he let Todd know that I certainly wouldn't be getting it all with him either. He said he thought Todd was being completely immature and selfish. Todd told me later that their conversation moved him deeply. He decided he was being judgmental, idealistic, and unrealistic.

A little over a year after his proposal, Todd called me on a cold day in January. Our conversation was light and casual. After a few pleasantries, Todd calmly asked, "Do you think we can do this by April, before the football season starts?"

"Do what?" I asked, confused.

"Get married."

"What are you talking about, Todd?"

"Can you answer the question?"

"Are you asking me to marry you again?"

"Will you?"

I was flabbergasted. "Let me call you back."

After I hung up and questioned his sanity, I called Delores.

"Dee, you are not going to believe who just called me."

"Todd?"

"Yes."

"What did he want?"

"He wants to know if I think we can still be married in April before the start of preseason!"

"What did you say?"

"Nothing. I told him I would call him back."

Delores and I talked for two hours. I wasn't sure Todd was really ready for marriage. He had assured me that he understood he'd been wrong to judge me based on my past, and that he was sorry for calling off our wedding. I struggled with the idea that one conversation with someone could change Todd's entire perspective. I feared he would change his mind again.

Delores agreed with all of my concerns, and she encouraged me to meet with Todd so I could look him in the eyes and explain my fears and lack of trust. I knew that was the right thing to do.

When I saw Todd, he again expressed that his conversation with his friend had helped him to see that I really was the one for him. I was still cautious; however we began seeing each other again regularly and talking for hours every day about the reality of marriage. Todd continued to press me to set a date, but I needed a little more time to be sure.

I didn't know it at the time; but while Todd was waiting for my answer, he was already planning our wedding—with the help of Delores! She had confronted Todd the day after she and I talked, and he convinced her that he was serious about me. He'd asked her to help with the wedding plans because he was sure I would come around.

While I was trying to make up my mind, I talked to Delores all the time. Finally one day, she asked me what I was most afraid of. When I said "rejection," she told me about all the plans that were already in the works. I was shocked but delighted. By that point, between her and Todd, most of the work was complete.

My mother had said, over and over, that it would be nice if Todd were the one; but more importantly, she wanted me to be happy. Finally I realized that I did trust Todd, and that marrying him would make me happy. After I accepted his proposal *again,* my father asked to meet with Todd. I never really learned what they talked about, but they spent nearly three hours together. Later, Todd told me how much he respected my father.

❧

Todd and I were married three months later, on April 2, 1988. The ceremony was beautiful. It was the day before Easter Sunday, so the flowers I chose were lilies. I walked down the aisle with my dad as the instrumental version of *So Amazing*, by Luther Vandross, played softly in the background. It was an evening wedding, and the glow from the candelabras set an intimate scene as we exchanged our vows before our family and friends. Todd's groomsmen included Mike Singletary, the legendary Walter Payton, and Shaun Gayle. His teammates' attendance made the day even more special for Todd.

The following weekend, we moved to downtown Chicago. We continued to commute to Columbus, Ohio, while renovating our newly-purchased home. We began to settle into married life. *It's so amazing to be loved ...* In my world, we were still on our honeymoon. Then one July day, the telephone rang. There it was again—another tap on my shoulder.

PART

3

9

'TIS BETTER TO HAVE LOVED AND LOST

I picked up the phone. "Hello?"

It was Delores. "You busy?"

"No, Todd and I were just heading out to get a bite to eat. What's up?"

"Nothing," she mumbled. "Just call me later."

"No, what's up?" I said, concerned. "I've got a minute."

"Well ... I found a lump in my breast."

I admit I didn't know much about breast cancer. And since I knew Delores always had her yearly mammograms, I figured this was no big deal.

"Well, what does this mean?" I asked her.

"I have to have surgery on my left breast, and I have to have a biopsy."

"When?"

"In two days."

"Do you want me to come home?"

"No, it's just a routine procedure. I'll have Marie call you when it's over."

I got into the car and told Todd what Delores had said. We talked about it briefly, then went out and enjoyed our dinner. I was not the least bit worried about Delores. She was the most levelheaded, in-charge person I knew. She was my hero. I depended on her then, just as I always had done. It didn't even enter my mind that there could possibly be something seriously wrong with her. I called her that night and we talked for more than an hour. I sensed fear in her voice for the first time ever. I decided to go to Chicago so I could be with her after the procedure.

She was already in the operating room when I arrived at the hospital. I sat in the waiting area with Marie, James, and Delores' boyfriend, Booker. When the doctor appeared, the grim look on his face revealed something was terribly wrong. We all listened as he told us that Delores was very sick. Her cancer was stage four, and all eleven lymph nodes that they removed were infected. The doctor predicted the cancer would spread to her vital organs rather quickly. He finished his medical evaluation, told us how long she would be in recovery, and walked away.

We were all in shock. I was afraid and in disbelief. Delores had *always* been there for me; she'd pulled me through so many tough times. A part of me dismissed the doctor's prognosis, believing that because of Delores' strength, she would be fine. But there was a voice inside my head whispering, *what if she isn't?* I pushed that thought out of my mind as quickly as possible. That was the beginning of my struggle with hope and reality, each one fighting to pull me to their side.

By this time, our parents were retired and had moved back to Jackson, Mississippi. We had decided not to call them until the procedure was complete. We all hoped and assumed that everything would be fine, and did not want to worry them unnecessarily. Oh, how wrong we had been. We decided we couldn't tell our parents over the phone; they were too many miles away and they were alone. So James decided to take a flight to Mississippi to break the news to them. We also had to determine how to tell Delores' daughters, Lisa, who was away at Howard University, and Anika, who was in the 7th grade. I arranged to pick up Anika after school and tell her myself.

Once Delores was in recovery, Marie, James, Booker, and I went in to see her. She was out of it, and she looked fragile and helpless. She didn't look like my big sister—the calm, reassuring one. She was always such a woman of strength. I wanted desperately to give her that strength now, but I wasn't sure if I was up to it. We were all in tears when we left the hospital. I don't know what gear shifted, but something rose in me that I still can't explain today. I became Delores' caregiver. I didn't choose it; it chose me.

⸎

When I returned to Columbus, I discussed with Todd what Delores was facing and asked him if it were okay to go back to Chicago to be there for her. I had no idea how long I would be gone. He understood and completely supported me. Todd considered coming with me, but he was incredibly busy at home. He wasn't playing professional football anymore, but he had just started his own foundation: Builders of Dreams for Youth (B.O.D.Y.), which consisted of tutoring, mentoring, and counseling at-risk high school students. Students applied for the program by writing a letter explaining their dreams for their future. If they completed the program, they were granted their wishes upon graduation. Todd was also on the speaking circuit, which required a lot of time and travel. Even though we were apart, Todd and I talked several times a day. No matter how busy, he made time to find out how things were going with my family. His concern for Delores and me was always heartfelt and sincere.

In the afternoons, Delores and I ate lunch together. She felt pretty good most of the time, and we could talk for at least an hour before she felt tired. We flipped through magazines and newspapers, and talked about the hottest topics of the time. Then one day, she said something much more serious.

"I want to appoint you and Todd as Anika's guardians," Delores told me. "I need to know Anika will be okay if something happens to me."

"Don't say that, Dee," I responded immediately. "You're going to be fine."

"I'm all Anika has," Delores insisted. "I need to know I don't have to worry about her while I go through this."

Although I would do anything for Delores, I never thought about being responsible for Anika and I was pretty sure I didn't want to. And although she and Todd had a good relationship, Anika and I had never gotten along very well. Anika had such a sarcastic mouth, and I was constantly in her face about it. Mom, on the other hand, was very sensitive toward Anika. She felt Anika needed more attention than her other grandchildren because she had been so young when her parents divorced (only eight), and her father wasn't in her life at all. I understood that was probably why Anika lashed out, but I couldn't stand that smart mouth of hers.

That night I talked to Todd about it. I expressed my concerns about my relationship with Anika, but said that I knew it would give Delores peace of mind if we agreed to be her guardians.

"Of course we'll do it," Todd said without hesitation.

And just like that, it was settled. Anika would come live with us upon my sister's passing.

❧

As I was changing Dee's bed one day, I looked out of her bedroom window and saw what looked like our Range Rover truck. It was! And it was packed from top to bottom. As I watched, Todd stepped out and started unloading the vehicle. He hadn't told me he was coming, and excitedly, I hurried down the stairs to greet him. Todd swept me up in his arms, and I suddenly realized how much I needed him.

"You can't go through this alone," he said, looking deep into my eyes. "I'm going to be right here with you as long as it takes."

"What about the business, your meetings?" I protested. "You're just getting started; you can't stop in the middle of everything."

"Everything else will have to wait. This is what's important."

Todd worked nonstop. He was my source of strength. This was not his family and Delores was not his sister, yet the love he showed us all spoke volumes. He never complained or made me feel as if I owed him something for his sacrifice.

My parents left their home in Jackson and drove to Chicago and we all moved in with Delores shortly after Todd arrived. Delores made it through chemotherapy and radiation like a champ. The treatments left her weak and very fatigued, but she didn't let it keep her down. I admit that I was very nervous when I first began taking care of Delores. I had never seen her down; seeing her sick rocked me. I wondered constantly if she would really get better or if she would only get worse. I prayed that God would allow her to live to see her children become adults. I couldn't imagine my nieces' lives without their mom.

One night after Delores had showered, I applied moisturizer to her scalp; and then all of a sudden, her hair started coming out in my hands. It overwhelmed me so much that I couldn't control my sobs. But I didn't tell Delores. I stuffed her hair in my pocket, put her bonnet on her head, and kissed her goodnight. After she fell asleep, I called Booker, asking him to please come early the next day to tell Delores about her hair. The next morning Booker came in with his bright smile and headed upstairs to see Dee. We knew he was hurting, like we all were, but he remained strong. I came up a short time later to go to my room and as I walked past the bathroom, I saw Booker in there with Delores—cutting her hair. When I came back past the door a little while later, the radio was on. And Booker and Delores were holding each other and slow dancing as he ran his fingers over her bald head. Delores had never looked more beautiful.

Delores continued to do well for the first three years after her diagnosis. We were holding on to the five-year mark. We knew if she could survive without a recurrence for five years, her chances of long-term survival would increase greatly. Each year marked a new victory. She continued to hold on to the hope that she would be able to see Anika finish high school, and she was determined to attend Lisa's graduation from Howard University. The day she left for Lisa's graduation was more of a celebration for Dee, as far as I was concerned. But shortly after she returned home from Washington, D.C., Delores got sicker. Her balance was off as she walked, and she no longer had the strength in her feet to drive her car. Todd and I had gone home to Columbus, but when I heard Dee was getting worse I booked a flight back to Chicago; Todd joined me a few days later. Delores met me at Chicago's Midway Airport; and as we approached each other, I noticed she was holding on to the wall for support as she walked. I took her by the arm and drove her home. She climbed into bed, and I made an appointment for her to see her oncologist right away. Further testing confirmed that the cancer had metastasized to her bones, liver, and brain. She was inconsolable as she wept in my arms like a baby. I knew I would be by Delores' side until this was over.

My siblings came by every evening. There was plenty of work to be done. We each had our assignments and we all helped as much as possible, if not more. Marie and my brothers covered the bases when it came to moral support. They made her laugh and kept her company, while at the same time, striving to hide their own pain. Denise was the only one we did not depend on. She excused herself by telling us she could not handle seeing her big sister in that condition. Everyone in the family disregarded Denise's behavior by saying, "You know how Denise is." I, on the other hand, was not that understanding. None of us wanted to see our sister in this condition, but now was not the time to wallow in self-pity. We needed to put our personal fears aside and take care of Delores.

As badly as I wanted to confront Denise, I decided against it. We still found ourselves at odds constantly, just as we had done when we were younger. We didn't spend much time together, and when we did, we argued over the smallest things. Our relationship consisted of little more than an occasional phone call and a casual conversation if we were in the same space. Sometimes we avoided speaking to each other altogether. I didn't know what was going on in her life unless I asked my siblings or my mom. But everyone was so upset about Delores at this point that I knew it was not the time to address my issues with Denise.

Daddy did not handle Delores' illness well at all. He buried his emotions and kept busy outside the house. He did all the shopping and yard work, paid the bills, and made the runs to the pharmacy. Mom stayed in the kitchen, cooking and sterilizing everything in sight. The doctor had explained to us that because Delores' immune system was greatly compromised by the chemotherapy, it was important that she be guarded against infection. My mom was on a mission; if you sneezed, you could expect a spray of Lysol in your face. Anyone who wanted to visit with Delores was handed a mask before entering her room.

Todd and I took care of all Delores' personal needs. We took her to all of her doctor appointments. There were times when she would be so sick and weak after a round of chemotherapy that we would have to rush her to the emergency room for hydration. On one of those days, Delores was shaking and I was trying to comfort her. She told me she was freezing. She was taken immediately to the back and put into a patient room. As she lay on the bed, she continued to complain about feeling cold. I snatched open the curtains and hollered out that I needed some blankets.

There must have been fourteen blankets covering Delores as we waited for the doctor to attend to her. Only her face was exposed. When the nurse came in to hook her up to the IV, Delores exposed one very thin, bony, bruised arm, which was so marked up from all the injections that most of her veins were fried. The nurse finally found a spot and began the drip to rehydrate Delores' frail body. As I stood watching, I wondered how much more of this she could take. As badly as I wanted to take her home and put her in her own bed, I asked myself whether it would be better if she died that day. I struggled with the guilt and shame of that thought; it was just that her suffering did not seem to have an end and I wanted her to be at peace. But it was not her time yet, so we returned home from another painful ordeal at the hospital.

⚜

Over the next several months, Delores fought to maintain her independence. It upset her that she needed help with her everyday existence. By that point, she was so weak that I would get in the shower with her to bathe her. This angered her more than anything. After tucking Dee into bed one night, I did not head downstairs to join my parents and Todd as I usually did. Instead I slipped away to my room and sat quietly, thinking about what had just occurred. I wanted to scream as I thought about having to give my sister a bath because she was unable to care for herself. I began to plead with God for Dee's healing. I felt hopeless, tired, and fearful; but I refused to give up.

One night as I slept, Delores made her way out of her bed and down the hall to the back bedroom that Todd and I shared. It was very early in the morning when she knocked on our door. I leaped out of bed to see if she was okay. She stood there crying. I walked her down the hall to the bathroom. As I wiped her face, she explained that the darkness was more than she could bear. She thought she was going to die that night, and she was afraid to be alone. After that, I never let her sleep by herself again. In fact, Todd was so understanding that he allowed me to leave our bed to comfort my sister in her bed as needed. Fear had its grip on my sister, and I was not having it. She and I read the scripture on overcoming fear. Delores began praying, meditating, and repeating positive affirmations about life. Her confidence soon returned.

One day, Todd noticed that I wasn't looking that great myself and suggested I lie down for a little while. It was the middle of the day, and I refused such silliness. I never felt tired! It didn't occur to me that I hadn't been getting much sleep. But that afternoon, I became violently ill. Pain was running through my entire abdominal area. I couldn't stand or walk. I called a friend of mine, Dr. John Hobbs, and I described the symptoms. He asked me to meet him at the hospital. He was waiting when Todd and I arrived. After talking to Todd, he had me admitted for testing. At least, that's what he told me. I later learned that he admitted me so I could rest. I slept for three days and three nights!

I made the mistake of thinking that no one could care for my sister the way I could. I was staying by Delores' side twenty-four hours a day; and though my intentions were good, it was not healthy for me—mentally, physically, or spiritually. One person cannot carry such a heavy load, nor should anyone be expected to. Thankfully, after my stay in the hospital, my strength returned. And I was ready to get back to Dee.

❦

Delores wasn't getting any better. She was confined to the bed and was unable to walk. Lisa was home, working her first job, and Anika was struggling with adolescence. She was only fourteen and dealing with an array of emotions dating back to her parents' divorce, not to mention her mother's cancer. She wasn't afforded the luxury that her older sister, Lisa, experienced growing up. Lisa grew up with both her parents in the home, when her mom was healthy, active, and very involved in her children's lives. My heart ached for Anika. But she dealt with all these traumas by rebelling. She reminded me constantly that I was not her mother whenever I attempted to chastise her. Having to deal with everything relating to Dee, I was always on edge and Anika's rebellion was a challenge. She was often disrespectful toward me, and most of the time I let it go and let Todd deal with her because my focus was Delores. But sometimes she pushed me to the breaking point.

Anika knew what her chores around the house were: clean the bathrooms, dust, and vacuum. One Saturday afternoon she asked my mother if she could go to a friend's house, and my mom quickly said "yes."

"Did you clean the bathrooms, Anika?" I asked as she headed up the stairs.

"I'll do them when I get back," she snapped at me. "Grandma said I could go out."

"Not before you finish your chores," I said firmly.

"I'll do them when I get back!" Anika shouted. "You are not my mother. Stop telling me what to do!"

When I got to her room, Anika was standing by her closet looking for something to put on. Without thinking, I grabbed her by the arm and pulled her into the bathroom. I held her by her shirt collar, lifting her feet off the floor. Our noses were almost touching, and I looked directly into her eyes.

"I know I'm not your mother! I'm not trying to be your mother! But I am standing in for your mother until she gets better. So you will do what I tell you to do, and you will not talk back to me ever again! Do you understand me?"

I know it was the pain I was enduring watching Delores suffer that caused me to lash out at Anika, but I couldn't contain it any longer.

"Do you understand me, Anika?"

By now, we were both crying.

"Yes, I understand you," she sobbed.

I let go of her shirt and apologized for grabbing her like that. I left her huddled in the corner of the bathroom. Anika was still crying when she went downstairs to get the cleaning supplies from the basement. I returned to Delores' bedside. Todd hadn't heard what had happened, but he followed Anika when he saw her tears. I don't know what he said to her, but Anika was in a much better mood when they came back upstairs.

Todd and my mother both had much more success with Anika than I did. I wish I'd known then that Anika should have been in counseling. Unfortunately, we were so caught up with taking care of Delores that we could not see Anika slipping through the cracks. Then there it was again—another tap on my shoulder.

⁂

One day while daddy was out picking up Dee's prescription, he called me to say he forgot what he had gone out to get. It wasn't the first time I noticed daddy being a bit forgetful. I mentioned it to mom, and she said she noticed it too. We both agreed it must be the stress from Delores' illness. But as the weeks went by, I started to pay closer attention. Something didn't seem right about daddy's demeanor. My siblings also rationalized it by saying it was just the stress. But I knew it was more than that; I could feel it in my heart.

So I made a doctor's appointment for him. I told him we were going because things were so stressful at the house that I thought he should have a physical. He thought it was a good idea. After daddy's exam, the doctor expressed concern for daddy's forgetfulness, but he also confirmed that the stress daddy was under was like having an eighteen-wheeler sitting on his back. He suggested further testing and referred him to a specialist for a follow-up consultation. He also gave him a prescription for Aricept, a drug that is typically used to treat moderate-to-mild Alzheimer's disease.

Sickness will either bring a family together or tear them apart. During Delores' illness, our family worked together in a way that brought us closer than we had been in years. We all coordinated, arranging our schedules to ensure that Delores was always cared for. To give us some breaks, Todd would bring my mom to our home in Columbus for a week, and then alternate by bringing my dad the following week. He and I flew home at least once a month for a few days at a time.

Delores' ex-husband's siblings were wonderful too. They visited often and were never empty-handed; they always brought food or money. Since Delores couldn't return to work, it caused a major strain on her finances. So we had a family meeting, including her ex-husband's siblings, to devise a plan to help sustain her. We totaled her expenses and divided them among us. There were enough of us contributing that it wasn't a financial strain on anybody. Everyone was absolutely willing to help out in any way they could.

Meanwhile, I was obsessively trying to force Dee back to good health by monitoring and controlling everything she ate and drank. I convinced myself that large amounts of raw foods, juices, and herbal products were going to cure her. I allowed her to eat only fresh foods, no meat, no sweets, plenty of fruits and vegetables, organic tea, nothing from a can or frozen, and definitely nothing fried. I read books on holistic diets, and whenever I went to the health food store, I always asked to speak with the person who specialized in nutrition. I would explain Dee's condition and ask what they thought would help her to recover. I even had someone come to the house to make a special tea that had to be drunk immediately. Even though I did not see lasting physical changes, it certainly calmed my fears.

Delores loved food. When she had an appetite and her mouth wasn't sore from the chemotherapy, she wanted to eat. One evening, Todd and I returned home early to find Booker sitting next to Delores, who was chowing down on a tray of fried fish, potatoes, and hot sauce. She and Booker looked as though they had just gotten caught robbing a bank. I didn't even attempt to take it away. I just walked out of the room, thinking: *Why am I doing all this? She does what she wants anyway.* Booker followed me and admitted that for some time whenever I'd leave the house, he'd bring Dee her favorite unhealthy foods. "Let her have what she wants," he told me gently. "It can't hurt her now." He was right. So I backed off with my strict rules, even though I continued to prepare raw food and juice for her.

During the fifth year of Delores' disease, she needed even more help. We couldn't leave her alone throughout the night, so we hired an overnight nurse to sit with her. Marie and I were spending more time together than we ever had, taking care of Dee's personal needs. It was weird. Even though I was grown, I still felt like a child when I was around Marie. The sixteen-year age difference still affected our relationship. I loved her, but she and I were never as close as Delores and I. Delores *showed* me what to do as a child; Marie *told* me what to do. I still viewed her as a mother figure and Denise was still absent, claiming she was unable to handle seeing Delores so sick.

Some nights, I would sit in Delores' room and just watch her. I remembered all the talks we shared, the secrets I had sworn her to keep, the uncensored questions I had asked her as a teen, and the raw answers she had given. I always believed Delores could conquer anything, but breast cancer was winning this battle.

By this time, the cancer had spread to her brain; and sometimes her speech was very slurred. She couldn't always get her thoughts together, and sometimes she could only lie still. She no longer had control of her bodily functions. All of her nourishment came through a tube. Delores was a very proud woman, and we did everything we could to maintain her dignity.

Delores was as comfortable as could be expected. She slept most of the time, but there would be brief periods when she was alert and awake, and we would talk and laugh. I cherished those moments. She looked at me one night and smiled as she said, "Daphne, life is a journey of laughter. Enjoy it."

Another night, she calmly talked about her funeral and what she hoped for Lisa and Anika. All of her financial affairs were taken care of. Delores arranged for her daughters to be financially secure as well. She asked me to do one final thing for her: get two copies of the song, "If I could," by Regina Belle, the R&B singer. She wanted me to give them to her daughters, along with a note she had written to each of them, as a reminder of who they were to her. She told me how badly she wanted to be a grandmother, to see Anika graduate from high school, and to celebrate her fiftieth birthday, but she knew she wouldn't.

We all knew Delores was losing her battle. The house was becoming lifeless. Delores was sleeping most of the time, so everyone spoke and walked softly. When my mom would disappear, I could always find her in her bedroom on her knees, praying and crying. Daddy often sat on the sofa across from Delores, staring at her with his legs crossed as he nervously shook his foot. *How will we make it through this?* I thought.

Then one day I came into the den, where Delores now slept because she could no longer climb the stairs. Delores' face was to the wall. I thought she was asleep, but then I overheard her softly praying: "Lord, take me into your kingdom." I left the room and fell against the other side of that very same wall; and cried out, "She's tired, Lord, she's so tired!" I whispered, sobbing. "Give us the strength to let her go."

Each of us spent our own time with Delores. By now she was sedated most of the time. She wanted to live, but this was not living. We didn't want her to suffer anymore. When the doctor ordered hospice care (the final stage of health care) we all knew what that meant. I think James was the one who then suggested we say our last goodbyes to our sister. Once we said our goodbyes, it actually caused a calm to settle upon us. I believe once we showed Delores it was okay to go, she was able to stop holding on for us. At that point, it would only be a matter of time.

10

LOVE NEVER DIES

he stress of sleeping in one of the smaller bedrooms in Delores' home, along with everything that was happening to my family, was beginning to take its toll on Todd and our marriage. Todd and I were still newlyweds when Dee was diagnosed, but we were the kind of people who jumped in to help when it was needed. When he joined me in Chicago, he did it willingly. The problem was that everything moved so quickly, and we never devised a plan to maintain our relationship while taking care of Dee. Our time with her made us stronger in some ways, but it was also the beginning of a huge host of problems that would plague our relationship for years.

While caring for Delores, Todd and I were not spending any significant time alone. For years, we had always set aside our Friday evenings for date night; but, we hadn't had time for that in months. I should not have allowed myself to feel guilty about enjoying myself while my sister battled this disease, and I shouldn't have put my marriage on hold to be there for my sister. There needed to be a balance to keep us strong as a couple and strong for Delores. But I couldn't see that then.

Todd and I began to nitpick about small things, which grew into bigger things, which then grew into silence. We argued about everything and nothing. For two years, I'd been neglecting my husband and placing my sister's needs above his. I made my sister my number 1 priority and pushed Todd behind her. Todd and I lost the romantic connection that had made us fall in love with each other. He would tell me he was craving some alone time for the two of us, but I didn't feel it was important because I was so caught up in my sister's disease. I didn't realize the damage I was causing to our relationship.

I took Todd for granted. He was always there to help me take care of my sister, but I was so consumed by Dee's illness that I forgot that Todd was also my family. My need to be there for my sister was greater than my respect for my husband. My desire to will my sister back to good health cost me the unity in my marriage. Even though it troubled me, I figured that Todd and I had plenty of time, Delores didn't; and she came first. That was a huge mistake. I failed to prioritize my marriage, causing us to falter.

I recall one disagreement that got totally out of control. I was in Delores' room, getting her dressed, when Todd knocked on the door and asked me to come into our bedroom when I was finished. I went and sat down with him, and then Todd expressed his concern about the distance he was feeling between us. I asked if we could talk about it later, but Todd sharply disagreed. Todd was not a man who communicated his feelings readily; so when he finally expressed concern, he had already reached his limit. I did not appreciate his tone and stood up to leave the room. As I reached for the doorknob, Todd grabbed my shoulders and spun me around to face him. I became enraged. My first thought was: *Did he just put his hands on me?* I felt like Todd's aggression was a mirror image of my past abuse. I told Todd to never, *ever* put his hands on me again.

After that incident, Todd did not speak to me for days. Out of anger, I in turn did not say a word to him. I was determined to put up a strong front, so I was as cold and distant as he was. But after days of not communicating, Todd and I found our way back to each other. We never officially called a truce; but one night as we lay in bed, our bodies, feeling neglected, did the talking for us. Then there it was again—another tap on my shoulder.

Mom and Dad took a flight back to Jackson to check on the house and get some business taken care of. Their neighbors had been so helpful. For an entire year, they tended to the maintenance of our parents' home, cutting the grass, collecting the mail, and so on.

I'll never forget, it was Wednesday, September 15, 1993, at 7:15a.m. My parents had only been gone a few days when the phone rang. As I picked it up, it was my dad's screaming voice on the other end.

"Something is wrong with your mother!"

"What's wrong?" I asked.

"I don't know, but something's wrong!"

"What are you talking about? Where's Mama?"

"She's in bed, and something is wrong with her skin! She needs a doctor, she needs a doctor now!"

I was totally confused. I didn't understand what my dad was talking about, and honestly, I did not want to hear it. I thought, *what now, God, what now? We can't handle anything else, not now!* My hands were so full with Delores; I wanted to hang up the phone and tell myself he was exaggerating. But I knew I had to figure out what was going on. I tried to pull myself together.

"Daddy, why does Mama need a doctor?"

"Because her skin has a hole in it!"

"Where does her skin have a hole in it?"

"On her breast!"

"What?!"

Finally mom picked up the phone. She calmly told me daddy was overreacting.

"What's wrong, Mama?" I demanded.

"Nothing," she said.

"Then what is daddy talking about? Why is he so upset?"

"He saw a cut on my skin while I was sleeping, and because he hadn't seen it before, it upset him."

My head was pounding and my voice was shaking. "What kind of cut, Mama?"

She told me not to worry and that I had my hands full with Delores. She reminded me how easily daddy could go into panic mode. She promised she would go to the doctor and call me later. I hung up the phone and tried to let go of the sound of my dad's voice, but his terror was too much to ignore. I felt like I had run head-on into a brick wall. I was temporarily paralyzed. My mind was reeling, and I thought: *This cannot be happening!*

I forced myself to push past my fear and call my brothers and sisters. A few hours later we were all aware of our mother's issue. I don't know who convinced her, but she did go to the doctor the next day. As I spoke with my siblings over the next few hours, I learned that the only one who'd had any idea about Mama's skin condition was Kenneth. He told us that mom asked him several weeks earlier if he'd ever had a tear in his skin that had a foul smell. He told her no and thought nothing more of it. Unlike me, Kenneth didn't ask any questions. I believe that's why our mom went to him. She knew Kenneth wouldn't pry, and that he would tell her what she wanted to hear. She needed someone to confirm that it was nothing to be concerned about.

I tried to calm down, to take care of Delores, and to wait and hear from the doctor. But my mind just would not stop. I looked at Delores and wondered if our mother could ever be this sick. Then my thoughts became even darker: *Am I going to die like this too?* Watching Delores die was hideous. I asked myself who would get in the shower and bathe me if I were sick. My answer was Delores. She'd always been the one I could count on, but not anymore. The rounds of chemotherapy that she had gone through caused a feeling of overwhelming panic that choked and smothered me. I felt selfish for focusing on myself as I watched Delores fight for her life and worried about my mother, but I could not turn off the terrible thoughts.

Normalcy. I wanted normalcy. I wanted my life back—back to the way it was before Delores got sick. I wanted to go home with my husband. I wanted happiness back, for myself and for my whole family. Delores' sickness had changed all of us; and if mom were now sick too, I could not imagine what that would do to us.

⁓

Marie took a flight to Jackson the very next day to be with our mom during her biopsy. When Marie called to tell us the news, we were all completely devastated. Mom had breast cancer, stage four, just like Delores. She was scheduled for a mastectomy the next day. I couldn't leave Delores, so Marie stayed with our parents while mom went through surgery. I spoke to my mom's doctor on the phone after the procedure. He told me that mom's cancer was very aggressive. So Todd stayed in Chicago with Delores and Anika, and I left for Jackson the following week. Because Marie needed to return to work, she left the very same day I arrived.

I couldn't believe this was happening. I couldn't believe I was on my way to talk to another doctor, in another state, about the same disease that had already turned my family's world upside down. I truly did not know if I had the energy to fight for my mother the way I had been fighting for my sister.

I took my mom to the doctor to discuss her treatment options. By then, I had become as numb as a zombie. I asked the doctor if I could speak with him privately. He said "yes," so my mom walked to the waiting room to wait for me. I was dreading the conversation, but I needed to know what my mom was up against. I couldn't look at Dr. Ruff as he spoke. I stood at the window with my back to him.

"Your mom is going to die from this disease," the doctor said.

"We are all going to die!" My tongue was very sharp. That word was consuming our family.

The doctor calmly said, "After surgery, she was so erratic that we questioned whether the cancer had already spread to her brain."

"So what's next?" I asked the doctor.

"Aggressive chemo followed by radiation."

Wow! I heard it all before. I stared out the window and thought of Delores lying in her bed in Chicago. Now my mom was sitting in the waiting room as we discussed *her* chemotherapy and radiation treatment. My family was falling apart.

❧

It was a good thing my mom had decided to have her breast removed. By the time they cut away at the tumor, half of her breast was gone anyway. The hole in her skin that my dad had seen *was* the tumor; it had literally exploded on her chest. I was so angry I could scream.

When we arrived back at the house, my mom and I sat in her bedroom as I shared with her what the doctor had said. I wanted to shake her. I wanted to yell, "What were you thinking?! You know what breast cancer is. You've been going through it with your daughter! How could you be so negligent?!" But I remained in control.

"Why did you let it go this far, Mama?" I finally asked.

"I was afraid," she responded.

"But you see what breast cancer is doing to Delores because they caught it too late! When did you find your lump?'"

"About a year ago."

"A year ago!" I exclaimed. "And you did nothing because you were afraid?"

"I wasn't afraid of having breast cancer."

"Then what were you afraid of?"

"I was afraid I wouldn't be here to take care of Delores."

I was speechless.

She explained to me that she knew if she addressed her lump, she would have to go through the same process as Delores, and that she would be too weak and sick to care for her baby. Her illness would affect Delores' recovery. She didn't want us, and especially Delores, to worry about her. So she decided to hide her cancer so that she could continue to be there for her daughter. She told me she'd planned to go the doctor as soon as Delores was better. Indeed, I was witnessing something I had never seen before: the full force of a mother's love.

We continued to talk. She told me the hole had such a foul odor that she had to wash it several times a day. She said that for some time she purposely did not get too close to me because she feared I would smell it and figure out what was wrong. But I never noticed a thing. My mother amazed me. The anger I'd felt quickly changed to pride, sorrow, grief, and joy. I told her that we would take care of Delores and that she needed to take care of herself.

Mom and daddy stayed in Jackson while she underwent chemotherapy and radiation, and Denise agreed to move in with them to help with mom's care. I was so relieved that Denise found the strength to be there for our mom. She never once said she couldn't handle it. In fact, I began to suspect that her absence at Delores' house was not because of her sister who was sick, but because of the one who was healthy: me.

With Denise's commitment to stay in Jackson to take care of our mom, I prepared to return to Chicago. Then I remembered that daddy had been scheduled to see the specialist. I asked mom if he kept his appointment. She told me "yes" and that the doctor suspected daddy had the beginning stages of Alzheimer's, but he wanted to order more tests before he could confirm it. After a long nine days, I hugged my mom; and then daddy drove me to the airport.

My brain was on devastation overload. Delores was nearing the end of her battle, mom was starting her fight, and daddy was beginning to slip away from us. The tears flowed as I sat on the plane, afraid of what the next moment would bring. Todd was waiting for me at the gate when I arrived in Chicago. I was exhausted. Delores' house was huge and eerily quiet when Todd and I entered. It felt as if death was occupying every corner.

I was so tired. My heart ached and I longed for some comfort from all this pain. I sat with Delores that night. I'd really missed her while I was in Jackson with mom and daddy. But now that I was back, the reality of how frail she had become was crushing. Delores, my sister, my best friend and mentor, was no longer there. Instead there was this horrible illness that had changed everything about her—her speech, her thoughts, her body, and her life.

❧

Our parents were able to come to Chicago to visit more often than we'd expected. Mom tolerated the chemotherapy very well. She never got sick or weak. She sometimes complained that she was tired, but that was it. She didn't even lose her hair; it only thinned out. She looked great, considering everything. During those visits, our mom was finally able to come to terms with the thought of losing her daughter. Mom saw how ill Delores had gotten, and she didn't want her to suffer any longer. Mom spent a lot of time alone with Delores, saying her private goodbyes and comforting her. Daddy had not yet said goodbye. I believe Delores held on as long as she did because she was waiting for him. Occasionally, when Delores was lucid, she would weakly call out, "Where's daddy?" Daddy was in the hospital; Delores did not know this.

One Sunday evening as Marie and James were preparing to leave Delores' house, daddy called out to James from the upstairs bathroom. Moments later, James called Marie and me to come upstairs. James looked pale.

"What's wrong?" I asked nervously.

"Daddy just used the bathroom and there's blood in the toilet, a lot of blood. We have to get him to the hospital."

Marie and I rushed to the bathroom. The bright red blood shocked us. James told us to leave so he could clean up daddy, and he said he wanted us to go with him to the emergency room. *What now?* I asked myself. James tried to comfort daddy as we drove to the hospital. I was speechless. No one said it, but we were all thinking the same thing: *Could this be colon cancer?*

Daddy was still bleeding when we arrived at the hospital; he was admitted right away. We quietly sat for forty-five minutes before the doctor appeared. I refused to look up as he approached. Instead, I stood and walked away. I was so sure it was colon cancer, and I didn't want to hear the doctor confirm my fears.

"Come back, Daphne," James said softly.

I wanted to yell, *Stop trying to force cancer down my throat!* But I didn't.

"Your father will need emergency surgery," the doctor told us.

"What's wrong, why is he bleeding, and what caused it?" James asked.

"His colon ruptured."

"Is it cancer?" Marie asked.

"No, it's not cancer. Your—"

We didn't even let him finish his sentence. As soon as we heard it wasn't cancer, the three of us started crying and reached out to embrace each other. We were so relieved, we ignored the surgeon.

"Thank God it's not cancer!" We rejoiced over and over again.

"Excuse me," the doctor politely interjected.

We apologized as we wiped the tears from our eyes.

"Your father does not have cancer, but his condition *is* serious. Cancer is not the only thing you can die from."

The surgeon explained Dad's condition and asked permission to perform the surgery. We were all smiling. The doctor probably thought we were nuts. Daddy was diagnosed with *diverticulitis.* As his condition worsened, his bowel had become obstructed and holes formed in his colon, causing the excessive bleeding. Surgery is not always required for this disease, but for daddy it was necessary. They removed several feet of his colon. The surgery was a success, but daddy remained in the hospital for six days. We decided against telling Delores that daddy was sick.

Then one night I went to Delores' room to check on her. It was close to midnight and the overnight nurse had left a few hours earlier. As I turned on the night-light, I noticed that Dee's eyes were open; but she didn't look right. I reached over her to adjust some tubing, and she grabbed my arm. She was unable to speak. I asked her if she were okay. She shook her head, no. I asked if she needed anything. She shook her head, no. As I began to lift her up, she grabbed my pajama shirt. I asked if she wanted me to stay with her. She nodded her head, yes. When I touched her hand it felt chilly. I asked if she was cold. She shook her head, no. I tuned in to her breathing: it had never been this weak before.

I knew my sister was in trouble. Delores' oncologist had given us his number to call anytime, day or night. When he answered, I explained that Delores' breathing was not labored, but was almost nonexistent—and that she felt cold.

The doctor calmly responded, "Delores is dying, Daphne. You know she asked not to be resuscitated."

"What should I do?" I sobbed into the phone.

"Make her comfortable," he said softly. "It won't be long." I hung up the phone and went back to Delores' bedside. I pulled the cover over her to warm her. I sat on the sofa and Delores kept her eyes on me, making sure I wouldn't leave her alone. I sat with her for more than an hour. I wanted to stay with her to the end. I truly did. But as time passed, I realized that I couldn't do it; I couldn't watch this. As I got up to leave, Delores made a sound, indicating she didn't want me to go. I ignored her as I ran up the stairs. I woke Todd and told him that Delores was dying, and I just couldn't watch it. He jumped out of bed and went to get Lisa, and the two of them ran to Delores' bedside. They were both with her when she took her last breath.

I was sitting on my bed with my knees to my chest, rocking back and forth, when Todd came to tell me that Delores was gone. He put his arms around me and said, "Daphne, I just witnessed the most beautiful thing I have ever seen."

"What?" I asked through my tears.

"As I held Delores' hand and prayed for her, she looked up at me and smiled, and just like that she was gone. It was sweet and beautiful. I saw Delores go from death to life, not life to death! She's at peace now, Daphne. I wish you could have seen it."

His words gave me the strength I needed to walk across the hall and tell my mom that Delores was gone. As Todd helped my mother compose herself, I went to wake Anika and then I called Booker and my other siblings. I don't know who called the coroner. I sat in the kitchen, unable to watch. Anika was sobbing; everyone else looked on solemnly as the coroner removed Delores' lifeless body. Cancer took away her strength, her determination, and her persistence. And now the coroner took away my sister, my mentor, my best friend ... my hero. Delores died March 14, 1994, at 3:10 a.m. It was four months before her fiftieth birthday.

❧

James, Marie, and I spent the next few days planning Dee's services. We chose a mauve-colored casket, and I selected a mauve dress and cream-colored jacket for her. Lisa styled her wig; and on the day of the funeral, she got to the church early to paint her mom's nails.

Delores was beautiful and vain. The illness had devastated her body, so I suggested we close the casket because I was sure Dee wouldn't have wanted everyone to see her this way. I was outvoted by almost everyone: Lisa, Anika, Marie, James, Keith, Kenneth, Denise, and Booker all thought she looked beautiful.

The church where we held Delores' funeral was packed. Family, friends, colleagues, and former students all came to say goodbye to her. As we headed to the cemetery where she would be entombed, the procession extended for a couple of miles. We had not expected so many people to follow us to her final resting place. It was wonderful to see such a show of love.

We all crowded into the cemetery chapel, preparing for Dee's body to be placed in the crypt. Dee's pastor shared a few words before the family was escorted into the mausoleum to watch as Delores' body was laid to rest. I was relieved that we'd decided to entomb Delores instead of placing her in the ground. Delores had never mentioned a preference. I suggested the mausoleum because Dee didn't like bugs, and I personally couldn't imagine her body in the ground. I think entombing her somehow made it easier on all of us. My mother later told me that if Dee had been placed in the ground, it would have been more than she could handle.

After the entombment, Booker came over to me. Hugging me, he whispered through his tears, "You put my girl away in style. She was a class act, and you laid her to rest with class. Thank you."

"Thank you for being there and for loving her. You were her heart." I spoke softly into his ear as I wiped away my tears.

11

NEW BEGINNINGS, NEW CHALLENGES

Anika graduated from high school in June, three months after her mom passed away. She then moved to Columbus with us a few days later. She was resistant at first, but she knew this was what her mother wanted. Anika's presence in our home changed Todd somewhat. He was very concerned for her, and she became the focus of much of his time and attention. He did everything he could to help her transition into her new life, and he became a strong father figure for her. She respected him and was comfortable with his authoritative guidance.

I, on the other hand, did not handle Anika very well. I thought I should walk gingerly around her, because it was important to me that she understood I wasn't trying to take her mom's place. Boy, did I drop the ball! I displayed no authority at all. I just didn't know how to support her emotionally. One of my greatest regrets was that we all didn't go to grief counseling. Anika was trying to become a young woman while struggling with her loss, anger, and grief. I was clueless. We all needed someone to guide us as we recovered and adjusted to life without Delores.

One good thing was that Todd's silent-treatment tactic, as a means to control me, stopped for a season. It was as if Delores' death had reminded him how short life was. Even though he still didn't communicate with me very well, he wasn't ignoring me when we had issues that needed to be resolved. Another positive thing that happened after Delores passed was that our family started telling each other "I love you" after every phone call, and we now always hugged one another before going our separate ways. We had never expressed our emotions toward each other in this way before, a behavior we had all learned from our dad. Delores' death changed that. It was a powerful unspoken change; even daddy who was emotionally "unavailable," began to regularly hug us and tell us he loved us.

After Todd, Anika, and I began to settle back into our lives, I realized I didn't have much to do with my days. Todd returned to his work, Anika was away at college in Atlanta, and I tried to busy myself with projects around the house. But after a few months of that, I decided it was time for me to return to work.

I worked in radio as a morning news anchor when Todd and I lived in Philadelphia, during his time with the Eagles. I knew I wanted to return to the news media. So I sent my resume and demo tape to several local radio stations. A few weeks passed and then I received a call from Frank Kelly, the program director of Sunrise Broadcasting in Columbus, Ohio. He wound up hiring me, and my career at Power 107 began in the winter of 1994.

My job was personally fulfilling, but I missed being able to travel with Todd when he went away on business. I also could not be there for Anika in Atlanta. She was on her own for the first time and was not making the best choices. I knew she missed her mother immensely as she watched her roommate and friends share their new experiences with their parents. Todd traveled to see her more often than I did, but I began to feel a great separation between Anika and me. Our conversations were brief and impersonal. She confided in Todd on some issues she was facing, but I was completely left out of the loop. Todd and I were both concerned for Anika, and we often discussed how we could best help her.

After a year and a half, I decided I needed to be available to Anika more often, and so I left my job until we were confident that she was able to stand on her own two feet. I didn't know anyone who had lost their mom as a teenager, so I was flying blind. But I knew I needed to be there for her as she struggled on her journey.

My mom and siblings offered their advice; but in the end, I had to deal with this on my own. Once I was more readily available to Anika, things did improve somewhat, but not nearly as much as they would have if I had sought professional help sooner. Anika did begin to get counseling while she was in school. The last two years of her college life were challenging and difficult, but she successfully completed her studies and earned her accounting degree in 1998.

Anika decided to return to Chicago after college, and she got a job with Deloitte and Touché. Todd and I found a condo in Hyde Park for her, gave her the down payment as a graduation gift, and helped her get settled in her new home. She and I were in a better place with one another by then, but we both agreed we still had work to do. She admitted that she felt she didn't need another mother; but she did need a father, which was why she clung to Todd instead of me. She didn't want to feel like I was trying to replace her mom, so she pushed me away instead of embracing me. But after Anika moved back to Chicago, we became closer and more comfortable with one another. So I decided I wanted to return to work.

During the summer of 1998, I was hired as a part-time fill-in news reporter with Metro News Networks. I covered news reports for four to five stations each day, following a time schedule for each station. I sat in front of a microphone and a board that listed each station's call letters; and when it was time for me to report the news for a particular station, I pressed that station's button and was live on the air with them. As soon as I finished their report, I pressed the button and was live on the air with the next station. It was a fast-paced routine for the morning-drive shows.

One morning I was filling in for one of our stations, Magic 98.9, and caught the ear of the morning show host, Brian Scott, a fellow Chicagoan. Brian was impressed with my reporting style and asked about me through his general manager, Charles Richardson. I didn't know at the time that Brian was looking for a morning show co-host, but a couple of weeks later my manager called me to his office to inform me that Charles Richardson wanted to meet with me.

I met with Charles, and we discussed the opportunities available with Blue Chip Broadcasting, the new owner of both Magic 98.9 and Power 107.5. It was a perfect fit for me at Magic 98.9, but it didn't last long: two years later, Cathy Hughes, owner of Radio One Broadcasting Network, purchased Blue Chip Broadcasting. I thought I would be out the door as a result of the new acquisition. There was no longer a need for our local morning show on Magic 98.9, and our entire show was canceled and replaced with the Tom Joyner Morning Show.

Then Charles and Paul Strong, the program director for Power 107.5, our hip-hop station, encouraged me to join their team and give it a try. I did, and to my surprise, I found myself enjoying it. The vibe I had with Paul created a chemistry that was not only funny, but also serious when need be. Our listeners often spoke of the connection they felt between us.

Each morning in the studio, Paul and our other co-host, Konata, would sip coffee while I prepared my news stories. Being live on the air is like spending time with your friends. We took calls and discussed community issues, hot topics, and personal concerns. I often continued my conversation off the air with women and teenage girls who were seeking advice. Our listeners really related to us.

Paul was a prankster. He never missed an opportunity to make Konata and me the butt of a joke. One morning we were off the air during a commercial break, talking about new hip-hop fashion statements. The phrase *bling bling* was just becoming a part of America's vernacular. Paul got up to leave the studio before the break was over, and just as he stood to leave, I casually mentioned the new hip-hop phrase *plang plang*.

Paul stopped dead in his tracks, turned around, went back to the mixing board and interrupted the music. "I'm stopping the music just for you," he told me. "Everyone needs to hear this."

He stopped the music, then turned to me and asked, "What did you say, Daphne?"

My microphone was on, so I had to respond. "What, when I said 'plang plang'?" I asked innocently.

Paul laughed until he couldn't catch his breath. When he finally recovered, he asked, "Do you mean 'bling bling'?"

The board lit up like a Christmas tree. Callers were laughing hysterically as I attempted to recover. This went so far that Todd heard about it at his office before I could even share it with him. When I got home, he asked, "What did you say on the air today? I heard you were off the chart. What happened?"

When I told Todd I said "plang plang," instead of "bling bling," he just put his arms around me and said, "My poor baby. It's gonna be okay." And we laughed hysterically.

Whenever I was out doing a live broadcast or making an appearance, someone was sure to walk up to me and say, "Hey Daphne, plang plang!"

Not too long after that, I approached Charles Richardson with an idea I had for a talk show for community-related topics.

He approved the show and left the details to me. I decided to call it "Eye on the Community." The show aired Sunday mornings, and featured guests in politics, government, education, and health. The show was successful, and it brought me even closer to our audience. I felt a new sense of purpose and a connection with our listeners as I gave back to the community.

My life was in a good place; things were going well. But I was finding myself constantly haunted by the fear of developing breast cancer. I would be driving to work, shopping at the grocery store, sitting in church, a restaurant, or the mall, and thoughts of breast cancer would flood my mind. There were moments when the fear would grip my throat so strongly I couldn't even swallow. Sometimes I would be live on the air, in the middle of a conversation, and the fear would hit me like a punch in the stomach. Sometimes just the sound of my mom's voice triggered it. If I thought about Delores, the fear would be strong enough to bring me to my knees. I was fighting a secret war, and the only way I could win was to keep moving.

12

FAMILY SECRETS

enise was still living with our parents, but she would stay somewhere else whenever Todd and I visited. She would call every day to check in, but wouldn't stop by to visit. And if I answered the phone, our conversations were very brief. She was as sweet as she could be; but I knew it was just me. If I was there with Marie, James, Keith and Kenneth, and their families, Denise laughed it up with our siblings. But she would have little to say to me. She and Kenneth's wife were as close as sisters. The disconnection between Denise and me did bother me. But because I couldn't identify the root of the problem and solve it, I didn't dwell on it.

One Thanksgiving, Todd and I, my siblings, and their families were all visiting my parents. During dinner, as we passed macaroni and cheese, turkey and dressing, and all the other trimmings of our family feast, one of us teased our father about being so strict on us when we were growing up.

"I never had to bail one of you out of jail, so I must have done something right," daddy responded stubbornly.

After dinner, the conversation turned to our grandparents. We often asked questions about daddy's parents. Because they both passed away when he was very young, none of us had ever met them. When I was a child, I remember hearing my father remind my mother that they'd made a promise to never mention some things from the past. That Thanksgiving, when I was in my mid-thirties, I discovered the secret.

It turned out that our dad's mom had an affair with a biracial man, a minister, who was married with a family of his own. She and her husband, the man whom I thought was my grandfather, were dark-skinned, and all of their children—my aunts and uncles—were dark as well. So when my grandmother delivered very light-skinned twin babies, the rumors started flying. When word spread around the small town of Starkville, Mississippi, that the reverend was the twins' father, he and his family packed up and moved away—never to be seen again. My grandmother's husband raised my dad and his twin sister as if they were his own. He never mistreated my grandmother either; he loved her and forgave her.

The secrets continued to unfold. My father's twin sister, Aunt Lois, whom he loved dearly, had six children. For the first time, I heard the rumors that she'd had them with four different men, none of whom were her husband. That revelation shed a lot of light on why my father was so strict on his daughters, and so critical of the young men who came to visit or take us out. If only he knew how to tell me he loved me and that he was trying to protect me, I'm sure I would have avoided many of the man mistakes I made. My father's family secrets embarrassed him so much that he never learned to blend his discipline with love. As a teenager, I remember asking my mother why daddy thought I was going to get pregnant every time I left the house. She had no response then, but now the answer had become crystal clear. Family secrets have a way of shaping your life.

After the discussion, daddy showed us a photo of his biological father. He told us that after he had his own children, he decided he wanted to know more about his family. So one day he returned to Mississippi to look for them. He knew that his father was dead, but his father's brother was still living. Daddy paid him a visit. His uncle answered all of the questions my dad asked him. After they talked, his uncle gave my father the photo we were looking at. Daddy never saw or heard from his biological father's side of the family again.

Mom had finished her chemotherapy and radiation and was doing amazingly well. It was almost miraculous. Her mental strength was incredible. She never complained and she never allowed the cancer to consume her. My mom was sixty-eight years old when the doctor told me she would not survive the disease. Today she is eighty-four and still doing incredibly well. God is good. I often tell my mom that I believe her recovery went so well because she attempted to sacrifice her own life for her daughter. I believe God honored her with life for that reason.

Daddy, on the other hand, was getting worse. He had become more confused and forgetful. The medication wasn't working as well anymore. Alzheimer's is a devastating disease. It robs you of your entire life. James spent a substantial amount of time with our dad, sharing his time between Chicago and Jackson. As the rest of us slipped out of our dad's memory, he never forgot who James and mom were. He called them by name, even when he couldn't remember anyone else.

Todd and I traveled to Jackson to visit my parents at least once a month. One visit was particularly painful. I walked into my parents' family room, where daddy was standing in the doorway. As I tried to hug him, he quickly pulled away; and with a harsh tone, he told me not to touch him. He said, "I don't know who you are, and my wife might see you. Get your hands off me." I attempted to explain that I was his daughter and it was okay if I hugged him, but it didn't matter. This was the strongest rejection I ever felt from my father.

We spent a week with my dad on that visit, and with each passing day his treatment toward me got worse. He would yell at me, curse at me, and would not listen to anything I had to say. Though daddy didn't recognize Todd either, he was very kind toward him—making it even more difficult for me to keep things in perspective. Though I knew it was the disease causing my father to behave this way, I still took it very personally. This was my father, the man who molded my thoughts, my emotions, and my life. This was the man I spent most of my life trying to please. Knowing he couldn't remember me caused my self-esteem to slip. Old feelings of rejection came flooding back.

Then just as suddenly as the unkind words had begun, they stopped. My dad still didn't remember who I was, but he was a lot softer with me. He hugged me, we talked, and he started telling me I was a pretty girl. During those moments, I would allow myself to forget my dad had Alzheimer's and focus on how beautiful his words were. I realized how much I still longed for my dad's love and approval, even though I was a married woman. I guess girls don't ever outgrow the need to feel love from their fathers.

Daddy continued to slip away from us. He was becoming more difficult to take care of, but before he became ill, he made us promise never to "put him away." We wanted to honor that request. Even though we knew he didn't know where he was anymore, he was still our father. So we all divided our time taking care of him.

Marie, who was now living in Jackson only a few minutes from our parents' home, stopped by every day. Denise shared her time between her boyfriend's house and our parents' home. She was our mom and dad's primary caregiver. She would take them to their doctor appointments, cook their meals, and help with the household chores. We were all relieved that she had finally become more responsible. It was also a great relief to mom. She enjoyed having Denise close to her, and it pleased her to see how attentive

Denise had become towards our father. With Denise caring for our parents, the rest of us could breathe sighs of relief.

All of a sudden, Denise began calling me on a semi-regular basis. I was a little suspicious, because we had never spoken very often. Now she would call and say that she didn't want anything in particular, just to talk. Our conversations remained light and casual for about three weeks. I was tempted to ask her why she was calling me so often, but I refrained. I knew something was up, but I figured she'd tell me when she was ready.

While she and I were talking one day, she calmly asked me about my menstrual cycle. She wanted to know if it was ever very heavy. I told her, "Yes, occasionally." Then she wanted to know how heavy and for how many days. A red flag went up immediately. Denise had never been one to talk about health-related issues. She was afraid of hospitals and didn't care for doctors. So of course I probed.

Eventually she admitted that she had been experiencing very heavy cycles, and she asked me to recommend an herbal treatment. I suggested she see her gynecologist first. She promised me she would. Weeks later, she told me she'd seen a doctor and received treatment. I asked if the bleeding had gotten better, and she said that it had. We chatted awhile longer and I didn't ask any more questions. I later learned that she didn't even have a gynecologist.

Things went back to normal for us after that, and we didn't talk again for several months. Our relationship remained the same as it had been for years: we loved each other; we just didn't like each other. On the other hand, Kenneth and I developed a solid relationship—despite his closeness with Denise. During one of our conversations, he mentioned that Denise was going to need surgery, possibly a hysterectomy. I was sad and worried, but I was glad she was getting herself taken care of.

I called mom to get more information about Denise's surgery, but she didn't really seem to have any. Denise spent a lot of time with her boyfriend, Roshea, so I thought he would know what was going on. But he didn't have a lot to say either. I understood why *I* might not know, but these were the people closest to her; how could they not have any details about her surgery? Something was not sounding right.

After the procedure, we were told that everything was fine and that Denise was doing better; so things calmed down. She and I spoke on the phone a couple times a week for a while, but I continued putting off going to see her. Then one day, James called me to give me an update. There it was again—another tap on my shoulder.

13

ONE LIE AFTER ANOTHER

enise was back in the hospital and not doing well. No one really knew what was wrong with her. She refused to talk about it, and insisted that her doctors uphold her patient confidentiality rights. I arrived in Jackson and my mom picked me up from the airport. While we were driving to the hospital, I asked her about Denise's condition. All she would tell me was that Denise had lost a lot of weight and didn't look like herself. Mom was so evasive that I knew she was keeping something from me. I hadn't seen Denise in over a year, so I didn't know what to expect. But, nothing could have prepared me for the way she looked. My once 150-pound sister, now forty years old, weighed no more than ninety pounds. I held her hand as I fought back my tears; so much time and distance was between us. The time in our lives when we were friends gripped my heart.

She smiled at me. And through her weak voice we talked about her condition. Our mom sat across the room as I asked questions I had become all too familiar with. Denise tried to tell me that her weight loss was just a result of her dislike for hospital food and a lack of appetite due to some medication she was taking. I pleaded with her to come clean: "Denise, don't lie to me. Either you have cancer or you have AIDS."

Denise was shocked: "Mom, please tell Daphne I don't have cancer, and I certainly don't have AIDS."

I looked up at my mom as she mumbled, "Denise does not have cancer."

"Really?" I said skeptically. "Then what does she have?"

"I don't have a disease at all," Denise said defiantly. "I'll be fine."

"Who's your doctor?" I demanded. "I want to speak with him."

"Denise won't let anyone talk to her doctor," my mother quickly interrupted.

I looked at my mom and knew for certain she was hiding something. This was a repeat of my mom's decision to keep her cancer a secret. Mom looked stressed and older than her years. I knew Denise had sworn her to secrecy. I was angry with Denise for putting our mother through something that was having such a negative effect on her. I couldn't believe Denise could be so proud and selfish that she would lie to me and our other siblings about the condition of her health when it was obvious she was terribly ill.

I took a deep breath. "Denise, would you please tell the truth, just this once?" I begged. "What is wrong with you?"

"Nothing," she insisted. "I had surgery, and I'll be fine"

"What kind of surgery?" I pressed.

"I *had*—I do not *have*—cervical cancer."

There it was. Finally she had come clean. "And what's the problem with me knowing that?" I asked.

"Because you ask so many questions! I knew you wouldn't let it go until you had every doctor in this hospital pinned up against the wall."

"Well, why didn't you tell Keith, Kenneth or James?"

"I didn't want them to worry about me."

"So mom has been carrying your secret all these months?"

"I had to tell her because I needed someone to take me to my chemo treatments."

I couldn't believe it. "You've had chemo?!" My head was spinning. I felt like screaming.

"That's enough Daphne," my mom cut in. "Denise is too weak to have this conversation right now."

I had so much more to say. Questions were rolling around in my head faster than I could think them through. But I made a huge effort to shut my mouth and let it go. I asked Denise if she needed anything from me. She said "no." Suddenly I was overwhelmed with guilt and sadness for our broken sisterhood. I took her hand and told her I didn't know where we had gone wrong, but I wanted her to know I loved her. I asked her to forgive me for my role in the breakdown of our relationship. She told me she was sorry and that she loved me too. We chatted a while longer, then mom and I left.

When we got back to the house, I was amazed to see how relieved my mother looked. The stress in her face had diminished, and the slump in her shoulders was gone. She was standing taller and looking like her old, vibrant self.

"Why did you tell me Denise doesn't have cancer?" I asked.

"She doesn't; not anymore," mom responded.

"Is that the word game Denise has you playing with her? Why have you kept this to yourself, with all that you're going through with daddy?"

"Denise asked me not to tell anyone because she didn't want to upset the family."

"But she thought it was okay to upset *you*, and allow you to carry this burden alone?"

I told her how relieved she looked since this morning, and she admitted she was glad someone else knew the truth. But I still didn't know the whole story. It would be a long time before

I understood the depth of the secrets Denise was keeping from all of us.

❧

During that visit, I went to see Denise in the hospital regularly. I paid close attention when her nurse or doctors came into the room to talk to her. If I was not asked to leave, I tried to gather any information I could from their conversations. But all I learned was that she had developed an infection, and that her current medication was not working.

One day, Denise asked what they were going to try next and the doctor responded, saying they were running out of options. Denise then asked me to go out into the hall.

"Denise, please!" I begged. "You do not have to go through this alone."

"Daphne, I asked you to leave. Please go out into the hall."

Reluctantly, I left. I paced the floor outside the door with thoughts darting through my head like cross-town traffic. *Running out of options* could only mean that they had tried several drugs on her already. What kind of infection did she have? What had caused it? If they got the cancer, why was she still so sick? I couldn't believe that she wouldn't tell me anything.

I was becoming accustomed to having conversations about life after death. I knew Denise believed in God, and she'd told me that she wasn't afraid to die. So one day I carefully approached the subject of her spiritual relationship with Christ. She admitted that it could be better. I had met a pastor in Jackson a couple years earlier and asked Denise if I could ask him to come visit and pray with her. She agreed. The pastor was very kind and spent quite a bit of time with Denise. He and I spoke often about her spiritual progress. During my next visit, she informed me that she had accepted Christ and felt much better about her life. As always, I was relieved to know her heart was right with God.

In addition, I spoke with my own gynecologist, Dr. Blank, about Denise's condition. He was stunned to hear my sister was dying from cervical cancer, a disease that is easily detected through a Pap smear and easily cured if caught early. He thought that Denise must not have had a Pap smear in years for the disease to have progressed to this point undetected. After hearing all of this, there could only be one explanation: Denise lied.

I discussed what I found out with Denise, and she admitted that she hadn't been to *any* doctor in more than a decade. She only went when she did because she was bleeding so heavily one day that she passed out on the bathroom floor. Her boyfriend, Roshea, had to rush her to the hospital. That's when she learned she had cervical cancer. Roshea never left Denise's side. He worked two jobs after she became ill to ensure there were always funds available to take care of her.

I wish I knew more about Denise's condition, but I didn't. All I knew was that the infection she developed could not be treated. Fluid was not passing through her body, and she was toxic because of the infection. She slipped into a coma; and after a few days, her doctor suggested we disconnect her from the breathing machine—the only thing keeping her alive. We waited until Keith could get to Jackson from Chicago. Not only were we still dealing with the fact that Denise had cancer, but we were also devastated that she was dying and none of us knew why. Everything, since learning it was cancer, moved rather quickly.

Numb, confused, and in disbelief, we all waited outside Denise's room while the nurses disconnected the machine and cleaned her up. We were told it would take about thirty minutes before she would expire, giving us all a chance to say goodbye. Marie, James, Keith, Kenneth, mom, dad, and I gathered around her bed. Daddy sat with his eyes glazed over, not knowing who we were or where he was. I thought for a moment that he was the fortunate one—at least he didn't have to deal with all of this. But then, I felt heartbroken that he wasn't aware his baby daughter was dying. From the time we learned of Denise's' condition to the time of her death, it took less than 30 days.

When the heart monitor stopped, my mother let out a scream so intense I could feel it in my stomach. As James held her up, daddy jumped to our mother's side and asked us to let him be with his wife. He didn't know why she was crying, but he knew she was hurting. It was as if his disease let go of him for just a moment. He heard my mother cry out and he knew it meant she needed his help.

Everyone stood there crying except for me. Because I didn't show my emotion with tears, I received hard looks from Keith and Kenneth, and later unkind words from Keith. But they couldn't know my thoughts. As I stood looking down at my sister's body, I remembered the times when daddy asked Denise and me why we couldn't get along. I remembered the many times he told us how it hurt him and our mom that we didn't act like sisters who loved each other. My answer was always the same: "I do love her. I don't know what happened." But as I stood there, I knew. I finally had the answer—pride. Our pride stood between us.

I remembered all the times we didn't speak to each other. I remembered the times we didn't say we were sorry for an argument. We were both too stubborn to admit we were wrong. We didn't agree on most things, but our pride would not allow us to agree to disagree either. It wasn't because our lives were so different; it was because we were more alike than I'd ever allowed myself to think. We were too proud to let the other one in.

Denise discussed her final wishes with Kenneth. She requested that her body be cremated and that her ashes be given to Kenneth. She also asked that we have a small memorial service for her in Chicago. Unlike my sister Delores' funeral, which was attended by approximately one thousand friends and family, Denise's home-going service was quite the opposite. It was attended by only a few friends and family members. Looking back, I realize my sisters' services were just as opposite as my relationship was with each of them.

When I think of Denise today, I don't remember me in her life or her in mine. When I think of her today, I fight the guilt that tries to overtake me because of the time lost between us. We were only three years apart and we should have been the best of friends. I wish I could tell her I've figured out what was wrong with us after all these years. But it's too late. Denise and all of our lost memories are gone.

It saddens me even more to acknowledge that if she had not been ill, I probably would have never told her I loved her. And even though I did, Denise died knowing I loved her because I *told* her, not because I *showed* her. What a waste. No sisters or no friends should be so prideful, or have anyone or anything come between them the way my sister and I did.

In the Bible, Proverbs 16:18 says, "Pride will destroy a person; a proud attitude leads to ruin." I thought of that verse as I stood in the hospital next to Denise's body. I thought, *I should have known better*. We were too proud to humble ourselves to resolve our problems, and our pride led to the ruin of our sisterhood.

PART

4

14

FINDING FREEDOM FROM FEAR

*I*t was 2003. Denise had just passed away, Delores had been gone for nine years, my mom was a ten-year breast cancer survivor, my dad had full-blown Alzheimer's, and my marriage was in need of serious repair. I'd been asking Todd for years if he would attend marriage counseling with me, but he wouldn't even consider it. As if all this wasn't enough, my own health—both mental and physical—was becoming a cause for concern.

Watching the devastation cancer brought to my sisters' and my mother's bodies terrified me. My life felt like a nightmare. I had been strong and supportive for Delores, but the combination of her disease and my mom's and Denise's diseases took my strength. Breast cancer changed me. I lost my confidence. I lost my hope. I lost *myself*. Death and sickness were like a shadow following my every step. It was an effort to have a normal life with my husband, but it was effortless to focus on my hopelessness. The laughter and joy was gone from my life and my marriage. Even though I was in excellent health, I allowed the disease to consume me. Fear eased its way into my mind and heart. I could not shake the ominous conviction that I would die the same way my sisters had died.

One final addition to my sorrow at that time was that Todd and I, after five years of trying to conceive, had to face the fact that we could not. The day we accepted this grim truth, a part of us died. We had to bury all the things that would never be, all the names we'd chosen, the plans we'd made, and all the unfulfilled dreams we'd spoken of so often. The day we left the fertility specialist's office for the last time, we cried until we could not see through our tears, holding each other's hands with all our might. It was devastating to let go of our dream, and it was very difficult on our marriage. Eventually God did help us to find the strength to let go and move on.

⁓

Due to my strong family history of breast cancer, I'd started having annual baseline mammograms. My last two had been abnormal, with cellular changes detected. After my second abnormal reading, I requested a biopsy. The report was negative. During a visit with my gynecologist, I mentioned that my breasts felt as if they had lumps in them. I didn't panic; because by then, I knew how a cancerous lump typically felt. Delores' lump was hard like a rock and did not move. The lumps in my breasts moved easily and I could shift them. I was diagnosed with fibrocystic breast disease, which is characterized by non-cancerous cysts in the breast tissue. Before my annual mammogram, the doctor drained the cysts of fluid because he feared a tumor could hide behind the cyst—causing the mammogram to miss it.

The condition can be painful, and it was for me. One day, I called Dr. Blank's office and asked if I could see him right away because the pain level had increased. As soon as I lay back on the table, Dr. Blank opened my robe, chuckled, and then asked me how often did I examine my breasts. When I responded "at least once a day," he said, "That explains the bruising." I hadn't even noticed that both of my breasts were bruised along the sides. I was rubbing, squeezing, and pushing on them so much that I inflicted myself with added pain. The doctor assured me that it was not necessary to do self-examination more than once a month. He strongly encouraged me to back off my routine.

As we sat and talked, I told Dr. Blank how terrified I was of getting breast cancer. I told him about the preventative herbal products I was taking and the reading I had been doing about the disease. He agreed that I had reason for concern and referred me to a physician who would manage my breast care. That helped, but it wasn't enough. I spent all my time obsessing about getting sick.

I read everything I could get my hands on about the disease. I joined a focus group. I met with a genetic counselor and had a family health history report done. I exercised regularly, and I made major dietary changes. My diet consisted of 90 percent organic foods; I eliminated most sugar from my diet; and I only drank filtered or distilled water. If I ate fried or junk food, I did so in extreme moderation. I began seeing a Maharishi Ayurveda specialist, an Indian doctor who specialized in alternative holistic methods for developing and maintaining good health. I began taking Maharishi Ayurvedic products, and I began a special diet designed for my blood type. I learned how to quiet my mind through prayer and meditation, but that only worked as long as I sat still. The moment I started moving again, fear gripped me.

My fear can be best described like this: Imagine yourself in a very dark place, so dark you can't even see your hands in front of you. You are afraid to move because you are not familiar with your surroundings. You have no sense of direction; so you stand still, hoping for a ray of light to guide you. That's how I felt all the time. Even though I knew God would direct my path, I was fearful. I knew the destruction breast cancer could cause, and I didn't know what to do. Todd was patient with me as I obsessed over the fear of developing breast cancer. He talked me through those stressful moments, and he wanted me to do whatever it took to find peace.

My Ayurveda specialist told me that the only way I would be free of this fear was to make a decision about my health. He knew that I had been struggling with the idea of having a mastectomy to prevent breast cancer. Even though breast cancer is the number 2 cause of death among women, such a radical procedure should not be the first option. For many women, it should not be an option at all. However, I questioned if it might be right for me.

One doctor I consulted advised me to play the waiting game by continuing with my annual mammograms and seeing what happened. But that just wasn't good enough for me. That was what Delores had done, and her cancer had been missed. I didn't know what I should do, but waiting for the other shoe to drop was not an option. I needed peace of mind.

I struggled with my fear and obsession with breast cancer until one doctor told me I was a time bomb waiting to explode. A full year passed this way, and it was time for my annual doctor's visit: physical, Pap smear, and mammogram. Even though the last two years of examinations had been abnormal, I was hoping this year I would have a normal reading—especially since the biopsy the year before had been negative. As I sat in my robe waiting to be called back to the screening room, I began having a panic attack. I had thought I would be fine, so I declined Todd's offer to go to the clinic with me. But now I was a nervous wreck. My hands became sweaty; I was lightheaded and terribly anxious. I'd been getting mammograms for more than ten years, but this time I was overcome with the strongest fear I'd ever experienced. I kept thinking, *What if it's cancer this time?* Even though I probably only sat there for ten minutes before my name was called, it felt like an eternity.

It was another abnormal mammogram. I was devastated. I didn't want to read another report about breast cancer and its link to family history. I didn't have the energy to consult with another doctor. I was tired of being tired. I knew I had to do something. But I didn't want to have surgery; I surely didn't want to have a mastectomy. I didn't have cancer, so why would I want to take such a drastic step? I felt extreme, like a hypochondriac. I reached out to a patient advocacy program through our local hospital. I wanted to meet other women like me—women who had a strong family history of breast cancer and who were considering a preventative mastectomy, along with women who were facing the same fears as I.

Eventually I found someone on the registry and contacted her; she was wonderful. We met several times. She listened as I shared my story, and I listened to hers. She did not have a strong family history of breast cancer; but she did have abnormal mammograms, just like me. She had several surgeries to remove breast tissue for biopsies, and they left her breasts so scarred it disfigured her. Finally she grew tired of the fear and the surgeries, and decided to have a mastectomy.

By the time I learned all of this, we had become quite comfortable with one another; so I asked if I could see her breasts. She was quick to agree. Her surgery had been performed the previous year, and I was amazed at how beautiful her breasts were. Yes, I even asked if I could touch them! Her breasts felt real, and they were perky. She looked great and she was very proud of her body. She didn't even have to wear bras anymore. Her decision was right for her, but I was still not convinced it was right for me. I wanted to talk with other women who had the procedure.

I met some great women who freely shared their stories. Each one told me that if she knew for sure that she was going to develop breast cancer, she would have a preventative mastectomy in a heartbeat. One woman told me my family history was a blessing to me—at least I knew what to expect.

I took a hard look at the situation. My family history meant my risk factor for developing breast cancer increased 80 to 85 percent. The surgery would decrease that risk to less than 10 percent. But even with my strong family history, it wasn't certain that I would ever develop breast cancer. I asked about being tested to learn whether I carried a hereditary gene. My doctor suggested my mom be tested first. If she carried the genes BRCA1 and BRCA2, my chances were even higher of developing breast cancer. But my mom tested negative; she was not genetically predisposed to breast cancer, even though she'd developed it. Her breast cancer, as in most cases, was random.

The doctor suggested that my father may have been a carrier, which could explain why Delores had developed the cancer; but her disease could have been random as well. I hoped for more definitive answers. I remained confused.

~⚬~

I decided I needed to step away from all things related to breast cancer and my breasts for a while. I had no sense of direction because I was so weary. Even though I prayed constantly for guidance, I knew I wouldn't get the results I needed because my prayers were filled with fear and doubt. I couldn't let go of *me* and allow God to guide my decision.

To escape it all, Todd and I took a wonderful trip to Aruba. We spent seven days on the beach, relaxing and enjoying each other and our time together. It was awesome for the both of us. We focused on the moment. I felt as if I were living in another world. When we returned home, I put my energy into my job, my church, working out, watching what I ate, and taking care of my body. Todd and I continued having our regular Friday night dates. Gradually, I eased back into my daily routine.

Several months passed and I had a breakthrough: I decided that I was going to lose my breasts to gain my life. I would not live another moment consumed with the fear of dying. My body was whole, but my mind was sick: *this* was in need of healing. Once more, I weighed the pros and cons of preventative mastectomy. I dug deep within myself and found the God strength that had been there all the time. I asked myself what I wanted, and the answer was *life*. I wanted to be healthy—spiritually, mentally, physically, and emotionally.

The moment I made the decision, fear lost its grip on me; and I felt peace like never before. I stood in calm silence. I felt confident and strong for the first time in years. I walked in faith, finally believing that all things would work out for my good. My journey to my decision was long and hard. We all have our own paths to pave.

⤲⤳

Before Todd and I left for the hospital on the morning of my surgery, he called me into the bathroom and asked me to stand with him in front of the mirror. As he stood behind me, he removed my robe. We looked at my naked body; he touched my breasts and told me, "These are not who you are. Your heart is who you are, and it is good." We prayed together, and then I got dressed. We left the house feeling excited about my life.

On the day after my procedure, the co-surgeon stopped by to discuss the results of my biopsy. It revealed that I had lobular neoplasia-LCIS. That's not cancer, but it is a marker of an increased risk of developing breast cancer. The surgeon told me I had definitely made the right decision, because he felt I was probably very much headed toward developing breast cancer.

All the doubts I had about my femininity diminishing and my husband no longer desiring me after the procedure were totally unfounded. Todd loved my perky new look, and I did too. He teased me, saying that as my body aged, my breasts would remain forever youthful—a bonus for him. But I still wear bras. I don't require that much freedom.

People always tell me how courageous I was to make such a decision. I was stunned the first time I heard that. My decision had absolutely nothing to do with courage; it had everything to do with life. I wanted to live. I saw what cancer had done to my loved ones, and I experienced the pain of losing my sisters. I did not want to live with or put my family through that experience again.

It was a long and difficult process before coming to the decision to have a mastectomy; in fact, it took eight long years. Even though the mark left by the incision is barely visible now, it will always be my battle scar. I have never regretted my choice. I believe it saved my life. It absolutely set me free.

15

A Thin Line Between Love and Fate

My marriage to Todd was often an emotional roller coaster. Six months after my surgery, our relationship was once again on shaky ground. At home, we faced the same challenges of every married couple. However, we both enjoyed traveling, and we were fortunate that we could take dream vacations pretty regularly. In the midst of our ups and downs, Todd and I vacationed as often as possible. Our favorite destinations included Aruba, Jamaica, Mexico, the Virgin Islands, and France.

One of our most memorable getaways was the time when we went to Rome. Friends told us that Italy had great designer clothes, shoes, and bags that were much cheaper than in the United States. But as we shopped in Rome, it seemed like the prices were not low at all. While we were standing in a Gucci store, Todd commented, "These prices are not any different than in the States."

An attractive Italian gentleman asked, "Have you been to Florence?"

"No, why?" Todd asked.

"Florence has what you're looking for, and the prices are much better than here."

The gentleman told us where the train station was, and Todd and I took the most beautiful scenic train ride of our lives. We were both enamored with Florence from the moment we arrived, and it became our favorite destination. The sights, the food, the people, and the energy drew Todd and me closer. We decided to stay that night, and we found a small but very intimate hotel. The lovemaking was exquisite. The next morning we awoke more in love than ever. The rest of our stay in Italy was wonderful too. Todd and I always reconnected when we were away.

But a few weeks after returning home, we fell back into the same pattern of disagreeing and arguing over everything. Our communication was at an all-time low. We would go to bed at night and everything would be fine; but the next morning for no reason I could determine, Todd would not speak to me. It was a repeat of our past. I internalized the silences as if I had done something to cause them, but I really didn't know what was on his mind. It began to agitate me to the point that I started to do the same thing back to him, until there was absolute silence between us. In addition, my sexual desire was diminishing. Things seemed worse than ever.

We were in trouble, and I wanted to save our marriage. Even though we attempted damage control, it just wasn't enough. Though our love was strong, sometimes love is not enough. We were in a rut. Nevertheless, Todd never neglected me. He did all the *things* a man should do for his wife (just like my dad). The problem was that I wasn't feeling emotionally connected to him anymore. But no matter how I explained that to him, Todd didn't understand my concerns. Telling him over and over again that I needed him to hear me, feel me, and reach for me was falling on deaf ears. I was wearing myself out expressing my needs. I knew Todd had to be exhausted too.

I'd been suggesting for more than five years that we see a marriage counselor, but Todd continued to refuse. He felt we should be able to resolve our problems on our own, and he spoke of counseling as if it were torture. I realized that on a subconscious level, he viewed counseling as an admission of failure on his part. His ego was bruised, and his pride would not let go of him. There were times when we argued more about our need for therapy than we did about our issues. I tried everything. I even went so far as to threaten to leave him, because I felt I didn't know how to be married to him anymore. But the more I pushed, the further away I drove Todd from the idea of marriage counseling. Todd had his pride, and I had my pain.

When he wouldn't agree to go to counseling, I had a totally different idea to get us out of this rut: I thought we could renew our marriage vows. I believed this would give us new passion for one another and a fresh start. I wanted to move out of our past and toward a new beginning. I felt as if I had just come up with the greatest idea of the year; I was extremely excited. It never occurred to me that Todd would not agree. Well, Todd not only declined my suggestion, but he also advised me to let all of it go. He said I should just concentrate on him and he would concentrate on me. He thought we should continue doing exactly what we had been doing, because he believed things would just work themselves out. With reluctance, I agreed to give Todd's solution a try; but within a few months, I had become extremely restless. The problems in our relationship had simply been covered with a Band-Aid, but the wounds were not healed. The little things, as usual, were getting out of control. We disagreed constantly.

During one argument, I threw up my hands and said, "I'm going to sleep in the guest room."

Todd was not having that. He followed me into the spare bedroom and climbed into the bed with me. He snuggled up next to me and said, "Goodnight."

I couldn't take it; I was livid. I turned the light on and asked Todd if I could just have some space for the night.

"No," he replied.

"Why not?" I demanded an answer.

"I'm not going to let you run from your problems," Todd responded with a yawn.

"But *you're* my problem," I answered.

"You've got some issues, Daphne, and I'm going to stay right here with you until you work them out," he replied stubbornly.

"What? *I've* got some issues?"

"Yeah," he insisted. "Whatever is wrong with *you* is what is wrong with *us*."

"Are you serious?!" I couldn't believe the nerve of this man.

"*I* haven't changed, Daphne. You have."

"That's the problem Todd; you *haven't* changed. We've been married for fourteen years and you have not evolved. You want me to be the same as always, so you can be the same as always and we can just go on as usual. Who we were fourteen years ago was fine, but we're older now, and different. My needs have changed; haven't yours?"

"What do you need that you don't have?"

"I have all the *stuff* I need; that's not what I'm talking about. I need you to understand *me*, the woman."

"I do understand *you*, the woman. I understand you are going through something, and I'm going to be here for you."

"What are you talking about?" I asked, leaping out of the bed. "You will not place all the blame on me! This is exactly why we need to talk to someone."

Todd remained calm. "I don't need to talk to anyone."

"Yes you do. We both do!"

"Turn the light off, Daph, and get back in the bed."

That was Todd: Ignore it and it will go away. Except it was not going away. I didn't know what to do. I didn't want to give up on our marriage. I loved this man, and I knew he loved me. But it was also becoming painfully clear that I had married a man just like my father: emotionally unavailable. I grew weary of my efforts to convince Todd we needed help, so I finally decided

I would just get some help for myself. I found a Christian marriage counselor and began seeing her every week. It was the best decision I ever made. It not only saved me; it would later save my marriage.

I walked into Dr. Karen Terry's office for my first session expecting her to tell me everything I needed to do for myself, and everything I needed to do to get Todd to come to his senses. I wanted her to be the black-and-white-shirted referee who blows the whistle and calls the game for *my team*. Boy, did I have a lot to learn! It was not her job to tell me what to do; it was her job to help me see things as they really were. To see *me* as I really was. It was painful and ugly, emotionally and mentally draining. I was forced to confront all the ways my childhood had shaped me as an adult. I had to face the fact that I was much more like my father than I had ever imagined. Over time, she helped me learn how to fix myself.

◦◦◦

I had been seeing Dr. Terry for about two months when Todd said he couldn't see any change in my behavior, and it didn't seem like my sessions were helping. When I asked him what he expected to see, he told me, "Anything that would make me feel like I was getting my money's worth."

Well, that set me off. Among other things, I told him that my sessions would not be effective as long as there was so much discord in our home, and that I didn't feel any support from him at all. We were still in a very rough patch. Even when we agreed to sit and talk reasonably, and to hear each other out, it didn't work. I told Todd we had been sweeping our problems under the rug for so long that the rug couldn't cover them any longer. We were living together as husband and wife, but whatever had worked for us in the past was gone.

Needless to say, Todd and I were not communicating effectively. Though he stopped using the silent treatment to control me, he reverted back to shutting down whenever we disagreed. I was struggling to own the role I'd played in creating the low place in which we found ourselves. I felt like I was always reaching out to Todd. I needed him to reach back, but it seemed like he never did. I felt like I was the only one fighting for the survival of our marriage.

Finally, one day our relationship crashed. The night before, we'd gone to bed angry with one another. That morning as I was preparing to go to work, I sat in the bathroom and said, "Father, I don't know how I'm going to do this. I really don't know if I *can* do this. I don't even know if I want to. But I know that I am in covenant with this man. I made a vow to You and to him, and I need your help if we are going to survive this."

I was willing to put in the work to strengthen our marriage, but I felt Todd wasn't meeting me halfway. Because Todd would not bend, we broke. I told him I didn't know how to be his wife anymore. I felt as if I was hanging on by a thread, and I needed him to grab me before I fell. All Todd heard from my words was that I was not happy with him. I asked him one more time to come and sit in on a few of my therapy sessions, so that he could get a better understanding of what marriage counseling was like. Yet again he refused. That was my breaking point.

"Maybe we shouldn't be together until I feel I am better with me," I said.

"Maybe we shouldn't," Todd calmly agreed.

I was shocked. Todd went on to make it clear that he was not going to move out of our home; and if I really felt I needed this, I should look for a place of my own. My pride kicked in and I wouldn't back down. You see, little did he know, I was an expert at being proud—as exemplified by my relationship with Denise. Three days later, I found an apartment a few miles away. While nervous and unsure about my decision, I felt like I had no other choice. Neither of us was handling the problems in our relationship well at all. Everything was becoming emotionally painful for me, and I needed a place to escape. I enjoyed being married and I wanted to hold on to my marriage, but I didn't see any way to go on unless we made some changes.

After signing the lease on the apartment, I phoned one of my girlfriends, another wife of a former National Football League (NFL) player, and told her what I was doing. Although she was saddened to hear how bad things had gotten in my marriage, she told me, "You are doing what the rest of us don't have the nerve to do."

Taking that apartment was the best move I could have made. It rocked Todd, and made him feel like he had lost control. It forced him to acknowledge that we really were in trouble. I lived in the apartment for approximately a month. During that time, I continued to see my therapist. Todd and I saw each other often, even continuing to go on our Friday night dates. The tension between us was not nearly as toxic. One night he inquired about my next scheduled appointment with my therapist, and asked if he could come along. His heart had finally changed and his attitude had softened. I didn't ask any questions; I just told him where to go and when.

I was the first to arrive at the appointment. I sat anxiously in the lobby as I waited for Todd and thought about all the years I had asked for this. I thought this would be the first step toward our learning to become friends again. I was so happy that Todd was finally open to getting help.

My expectations were obviously too high. As we took our seats to begin our session, Dr. Terry's first question was, "Why are you here, Todd?"

"I want Daphne to keep her mouth shut!" Todd responded angrily.

I was stunned. At that point, I had been in counseling for more than a year; and I had learned, first and foremost, that it's about *you*. I realized how much Todd had to learn.

Counseling was very painful for us in the beginning. It was not easy for Todd to let go of who he was. Dr. Terry even suggested that he seek someone else to speak with one-on-one, and to my surprise, he did just that. If he didn't talk to me about his individual therapy sessions, I didn't ask. I stepped back and let him have his space. When he did share, I learned it was better to listen and be his shoulder to lean on than to interject my opinion.

It was a struggle for Todd, but after the first few sessions, he began to let his defenses down. We both learned so much about each other during those sessions. We learned childhood family secrets about one another. We dealt with how each of our pasts had shaped the relationship we now lived in. We came to see that Todd and I played a constant game of *tit for tat* within our marriage. We both agreed that we wanted to be better, do better. The therapist gave us weekly homework assignments, and Todd was always the first one to set aside time for us to work on them.

It was sometimes difficult to watch as Todd released himself. I discovered that my husband was in as much pain as I was—if not more. Todd had to be in control of everything. He did everything he could to protect himself from being hurt or rejected. I thought back to so many years ago when Todd had asked me to marry him by writing a note: he was protecting himself from rejection by not asking me out loud.

While Todd and I were in counseling, I didn't feel criticized or defensive. Our sessions taught me that I was emotionally unavailable as well. I was also a product of my environment. I learned that I used my detachment from my father as a weapon to protect my feelings. If Todd ever said anything that sounded negative, I viewed it as criticism and became very defensive. I was responding to Todd in the same manner I did with my dad. My dad was always very critical of me as a child, and I learned to protect myself by becoming defensive toward him. That's how I treated Todd for most of our marriage. I felt he was critical of me and I became defensive, making it impossible for me to embrace the help he was offering. My past shaped my life until I knew better.

As our sessions continued, I learned who Todd really was: a man who was wounded and scarred. The silent treatment was a part of that. His silence was how he expressed his anger, how he dealt with his hurt and pain. I began to understand why he had struggled for so long with the idea of counseling. It meant he had to become someone he had never been—a man who expresses himself.

Todd told me one night that he never actually opposed counseling; it was the pain of having to relive his childhood that had held him back. Although we had been married for almost sixteen years, he said there were things he never wanted me to know about his past; and he knew counseling would mean putting it all on the table. Finally, he agreed that letting it out was freeing.

"Before Daphne and I were married," he said during one session, "I felt manipulated by some of those closest to me. I didn't always feel appreciated, even when I was giving from my heart."

As I sat and listened to my husband's words, I could not stop my tears. My heart ached as Todd expressed how deep his hurt was, and how he subconsciously guarded his heart because of his fear of old wounds—just like me. Todd's past had followed him into that office—just like me. And just like me, Todd's healing began in that office.

I had already learned that I could not be good for my husband or our life together, unless I took care of me first. When I took the apartment, Todd felt I had abandoned him. I explained that I hadn't been abandoning him; I'd been saving me. He eventually began to understand my position and stopped making accusations about the move. Slowly, things were turning around for us. I was learning to accept Todd as he was, and he was doing the same with me.

One of our most defining moments came as we were leaving the therapist's office one day. Dr. Terry looked at both of us and said, "There is so much passion between you two. You love each other; you just need to learn how to dance to a different tune with one another." She explained that we each knew how to push the other's buttons, and how important it was for each of us to discover positive ways of making the other respond.

We were finally facing our problems and actively working to resolve issues we had ignored for years. I finally felt like I could live the rest of my life with this man, faults and all. I asked him to forgive me for the anger I expressed toward him, and he asked me to forgive him for not trusting me with his heart. After all the changes we had endured, I knew I could breathe again. We'd spent so much of our marriage taking care of others, and now we needed to take time for ourselves. I knew things would be better now. I was so excited about our future. But there it was again—another tap on my shoulder.

16

WHAT A DIFFERENCE A DAY MAKES

March 16, 2005, started like every other day. Todd lightly caressed my back to wake me after the alarm went off at 3:30 a.m. After I showered, Todd threw the covers off, put on his workout clothes, and headed downstairs to make breakfast for me. He did that every morning. I don't even remember why he started doing it; I never asked him to. But I certainly never asked him to stop either! My mom taught her daughters to appreciate the kindness of their husbands. She explained that if our husbands didn't feel our appreciation, they would simply stop trying to please us. Preparing my breakfast, grabbing my bag, and starting my car for me gave Todd a sense of pride; I suppose. Plus, he was a great cook who loved to show off his skills. I really did appreciate his kindness. I'm so thankful I heeded my mother's advice.

That morning, after Todd brought my bag into the car, he said "see you later" as he headed out for his morning run. I was late and didn't have time to eat the breakfast he'd made, and I wasted no time leaving shortly after him. I arrived at the station with only fifteen minutes to spare before my first headlines newscast at 5:50 a.m.

At 6:50 a.m., my co-host and I were sitting in the studio during a commercial break. I was about forty seconds out from doing my next newscast when the hotline phone rang. My co-host, Paul Strong, answered the call on speakerphone. I wasn't paying attention, but I heard a voice say, "This is the Reynoldsburg Police Department. Does Daphne Bell work there?"

Paul replied, "Yes."

"Is she with you now?" the officer asked.

"Yes."

"Please ask her to leave the room."

By now I was looking at Paul, and he was looking at me. We were both confused.

"I think she said you should leave for a moment," Paul said.

I was thinking, *What do they want? Did I run a red light or something and they're trying to track me down?* I shook my head, and stayed where I was. Big mistake.

The patrolwoman said, "There's been an accident involving a fatality with Todd Bell."

Everything began to blur. My head started spinning, and the word *fatality* rang louder and louder in my head. Paul was asking questions, and it seemed like forever before he hung up. I remember standing up and looking at Paul, asking, "What did she say, Paul? *What did she say?*" Paul came toward me as I hit the floor. He told me later that I emitted a sound that kept him awake for nights afterward, the sound of pain coming from deep within my soul. He said it reminded him of a wounded animal.

Paul picked me up off of the floor and led me to my office. I pleaded with him to call a police officer friend of ours to find out what was going on. I picked up the phone and left a message for Todd to please call me immediately. I was crying, shaking, and totally numb. My brain couldn't make sense of the words I heard. I didn't know what to do, where to go. All I knew was that

I wanted someone to get me out of this. I wanted to run to Todd, but I didn't know where he was or what happened.

I was losing it. I kept trying to pull it together, but I was unable to do so. Finally an officer arrived. As I stood to greet him, my legs gave out. He looked like the enemy and not like someone who was there to help. I didn't want to speak with him. I was terrified to hear what he had to say.

"Mrs. Bell, I'm here to escort you to the hospital. Your husband was involved in an accident. He suffered a massive heart attack."

I stood up. I reached for the wall before I fell again. Surely he couldn't be talking about Todd! Todd was the healthiest person I knew. He was only forty-six years old. He'd left home for his daily run this morning at 5:10 a.m. Now the officer was telling me he died of a massive heart attack? My head couldn't hold any more. My brain hit the OFF switch, shutting all the words out. I could only focus on one thought: *This couldn't be!*

The ride to the hospital took forever. I was expecting blaring sirens and a high-speed drive, but the officer was driving so slowly I wanted to scream. I held my head down and kept my eyes closed as he told me the whole story. Todd lost consciousness while driving, causing his SUV to crash into a house. He didn't suffer any injuries, and thankfully no one else was hurt. When the paramedics arrived, Todd's pulse was very weak; so they administered CPR before rushing him to the hospital. The emergency-room doctors worked on Todd for more than an hour.

I just couldn't make sense of it. A heart attack! How in the world had Todd died of a heart attack? He'd just had his physical three weeks earlier. He was in terrific health. I couldn't process any of this. I took out my cell phone with shaking hands and called my brother, James. Next, I called my pastor, Howard Tillman and asked him to meet me at the hospital. I didn't say that Todd died; I refused to acknowledge it.

As we approached the hospital in the police car, I thought about how many times Todd and I had sat in that emergency room. I played out the scene in my head and thought: *If the doctor meets me at the door, there's a chance Todd is okay. If the hospital chaplain is waiting for me ...* I shut that thought out.

As I entered the emergency room, there he was: the hospital chaplain. I gasped for breath. I thought I was going to faint. I wanted to walk past him to ask the receptionist where I could find my husband. But I knew it was too late for that. I didn't want to go to the chaplain's office. I didn't want to hear his condolences. I wanted to go find Todd and take his hand and bring him home. I wanted to get us out of this place. As the chaplain led me down the corridor, he didn't say a word. When we got to the door, all he said was, "Your husband is in there." He walked away and left me standing alone. I couldn't go in. My feet would not move. I turned and walked back to the front of the hospital. I stood and watched patients coming in, doctors and nurses laughing and talking. I wanted to scream. How could they carry on like this while my husband was lying on a table—lifeless?

Pastor Tillman arrived minutes later. I asked him to go in to see Todd first. I was standing outside the door when he came out. He was speechless. Then he opened the door for me to enter the room. I slowly walked to the table. Here lay my husband: the loving and virile man to whom I had said "see you later" only a few hours before. Other than the tube in his mouth and a small mark on his forehead where his head hit the windshield, he looked as if he were sleeping. He was wearing his workout clothes, along with his favorite wool cap that was hanging off the top of his head. I wanted to remove it; but decided to let him be, resting peacefully. I reached out to touch his face; he was already chilled, not cold, but cool to the touch.

One day Todd had joked that if he died before me, I was not to just give up and let him go. He said, "Do me like Lazarus in the Bible; lay hands on me and order me to take up my bed and walk!" Pastor Tillman was standing behind me, and as I remembered those words, I seriously considered asking him to lay hands on Todd. I was desperate, but I decided against it.

My girlfriend, Edie, met me at the hospital and she drove me home after I officially identified Todd's body. We sat quietly in my family room. A short time later, Frankie Coleman, our mayor's wife, showed up. She stretched her arms wide to greet me. My head was throbbing. I wanted to sleep; but I couldn't rest. I wanted Todd to walk through the door and wake me from this awful nightmare.

By noon, the news of his death was all over the television and radio stations. Edie called my doctor to tell him I wasn't being very responsive, so he prescribed a sedative. It left me numb, but that was fine with me. All I knew was that I didn't want to feel any more pain. The next few days my mind was simply filled with the haze of disbelief and utter dismay. I wasn't even a big part of making the arrangements; my church family, friends, and family members stepped in and took the entire load off me. Though I did want to do one thing: I wanted to choose Todd's clothes and the color of his casket.

James stood with me in Todd's closet as I chose a black suit, white shirt, silver tie, and a white handkerchief. I wanted Todd to look as fine as he always did. When we met with the funeral director, I chose a silver and black casket. When I saw Todd's body the night before the funeral services, he looked so peaceful. He was as handsome as the day I met him. However, when I touched him, the only part of him that still felt like Todd was his hair. I stood for a few minutes, rubbing his hair and remembering his concern for his thinning hairline, which was visible now. I had often teased him about embracing his age more gracefully. He used to say that he planned to live as close to forever as he could, and he wanted to take his hair along with him. I smiled to myself as I thought about how he painstakingly took care of his hair.

The morning of the funeral, I awoke feeling very ill. I wondered if I would be strong enough to make it through the services. I was heavily medicated and don't recall much. I know I was the last one to enter the church sanctuary, and I sat in the church's waiting room with my brother, James and my girlfriends,

Edie, Nikol, and Melanie until the casket was closed. I wanted an open casket because so many friends, family, and loved ones had come to say goodbye to Todd and to see him one last time; but I knew I could not look at him in front of the crowd. I knew I wouldn't have been able to hold myself together, and I didn't want to have to be carried out before the services were over.

The church was filled to capacity. I was told at least three thousand people walked past Todd's coffin. I thought how I couldn't wait to tell Todd how many people had come out just for him. I still expected him to walk in and sit down beside me.

Mike Singletary officiated the services and our friend, gospel-recording artist Vanessa Bell Armstrong, sang a few songs. Columbus Mayor Michael Coleman delivered the opening remarks. Our pastor and friend from Philadelphia, Bishop Ronald Young, offered words of comfort, and so did Dr. Mac Stewart, Todd's boss from Ohio State University. Cris Carter shared stories of their childhood and the professional and personal relationship he had with Todd.

As I sat in a fog, barely aware of my surroundings, my eyes were drawn to the casket. I couldn't believe that my husband was in that box. After Pastor Tillman delivered the eulogy, the services were over. Todd's parents were escorted out first, and then other family members began to follow. As I stood waiting to join the procession, an usher gently touched my arm. She said she was going to lead me out the side door and down the stairs to avoid the crowd. She led me out of the sanctuary toward the area where the repast would be held. Family and friends continued the procession down the center aisle of the church outside the door to the foyer. The hearse was waiting to transport my husband's body to the airport.

The repast was held in the area of the church where those who were not able to sit inside the sanctuary had viewed the funeral services on a screen. I remembered being there during happier occasions: concerts, conferences, and other church activities. The room was set up with rows of tables and chairs, and the food was served from our church kitchen. A plate of food was placed in front of me, but I had no desire to eat. For hours, people approached me to express their condolences. I appreciated their show of love, but I could barely respond.

After the repast, family and friends started the drive to Chicago in order to attend the burial service the next day. Anika remained to accompany me on the flight to Chicago the following morning, along with Edie.

When Anika and I were alone in my very quiet home that evening, she kept me company and spoke to me as I packed.

"I didn't say goodbye to Todd until his funeral was over at the church today," she told me.

"What do you mean?" I asked.

She said she had placed one hand on the glass door of the hearse and waved with her other hand. Then she stood and watched as the driver slowly pulled away, carrying the only man she had ever looked up to as a father until it was no longer in sight. That was when she understood that Todd was gone forever.

❧

It was a rough night. Anika slept in the bed with me, but neither of us rested. The next morning when I opened my eyes, I thought: *Today is the day I bury my husband.* The nightmare was still happening. As I showered and dressed, I thought about how I didn't want to get on the plane, and I didn't want to go to Chicago. During the ride to the airport, the fog of grief rested heavily upon me. I stared out of the window as the plane began to taxi down the runway. Once we were airborne, Edie began to talk to me. She knew just what to do, tenderly keeping me engaged in light and casual conversation. The next thing I knew, we were landing.

James met us at the airport, and we drove directly to the cemetery. It wasn't long before we were all gathered in the chapel to say our final goodbyes. Almost eleven years ago, I stood in this very same spot burying my sister. My sorrow was insurmountable. Todd's former teammates began to arrive to say their final goodbyes. Each one spoke from their heart as they remembered Todd. Then our friend, Bishop Horace Smith, offered final remarks, prayed, and concluded the service. He instructed everyone to head toward the mausoleum. As I stood to leave the chapel, James stopped me.

"Daphne, I have been with you since the day Todd died, and I know you have not said goodbye to him. This is it. You have to say goodbye now."

"It's okay, James." I resisted.

"Daphne, you will regret it later if you don't do this." He took a chair and set it beside Todd's open coffin. "Have a seat and spend a few moments with your husband," he said gently. I didn't have any words. I merely straightened the handkerchief in Todd's suit-jacket pocket. Then I kissed him for the first time since his passing. His cold and hard lips broke my heart.

I believe that when our spirit leaves our body, we do go to a better place; we rest in the presence of our Father. I had always feared dying; but the day Todd left this earth, my fear left too. Todd left this earth like the man he was: strong and vibrant. He led a spiritually and naturally healthy life. He was focused and sure. He knew what he wanted, set his goals, and established the way to accomplish them. He loved life, he laughed, he loved people, he cared, and he helped. He lived by what he believed; he stood by his convictions. Todd had a way of making everyone around him want to do better—to be a better person.

If I had only known—as Todd sat laughing, talking, and listening to his favorite music the night before he passed away—that the remainder of his life would consist of only five hours and fifty-three minutes. If I had only known when he walked out the door that morning that I would never see him alive again. If I had only known when he said "see you later," that he was really saying goodbye. If I had known, what would I have done differently? I would have told him I loved him. I would have hugged him. I would have taken a moment to stop and look at him and to let him know how much I appreciated him. If I had only known!

As I sat there, I thought: *I'm sorry, I'm sorry, I'm sorry, I'm so sorry, Todd.* I repeated it over and over again to myself as I stared at my husband's body for the last time.

17

THE PAIN DIDN'T KILL ME

*I*t had been two weeks since Todd's death. The bed had become a refuge, a safe haven, my place to hide and to escape from my pain, hurt, disappointment, anger, guilt, and overwhelming grief. I didn't get much sleep; I lay awake consumed with thoughts of Todd.

Our wedding anniversary was a few days away. Our plans had already been in the works. Because we had been communicating well and getting along so much better lately, I had wanted to make our anniversary memorable. I'd booked a private suite at a lodge about an hour from Columbus. It was perfect … no television, no phone, not even a newspaper. Todd had asked that we not tell anyone where we were going, and that we both be prepared to discuss our long-term goals and plans for our relationship. I was looking forward to just being with Todd, a feeling I hadn't felt in so long.

Instead I was lying there, consumed with sorrow and unable to get out of bed. I wanted to let go of the idea of what was supposed to be and live in the reality of my life, but I couldn't. My heart and mind were fighting a losing battle. I could still hear Todd telling me how much he wanted our marriage to work; how glad he was that he had finally agreed to counseling; and that even though he knew we still had a lot of work to do on our marriage, he was up to the task. I trusted him. I missed him so much.

I was totally empty. I didn't care about anything. As close as I had been to Delores and despite the pain I felt when I lost her and Denise, it didn't compare to the pain of losing my friend, husband, and soul mate. Losing Todd was like losing a part of my soul; I could not imagine maintaining my life without him.

I understand we are all going to leave this earth one day. I was not asking: *Why Todd?* I was asking: *Why now?* Why, when we were on the road to recovery? Why, when we had finally both agreed to accept each other as we were? Why, when I finally knew I could live the rest of my life with this man? Why, just when I felt I understood what it would take to make our marriage work? Why, when we were both so hopeful about our future? Why not during the time when I was so angry and disconnected from him? Why not during the times when we didn't like each other? Why not then? Why did we get so close, only to have it all be taken away?

I knew I needed to talk to someone in order to sort through the pain, and to make some sense of the hole Todd's death had left in my soul. I knew what I needed to do. I knew I had to get help to get past the pain and start to heal, but I was frozen.

❧

I decided to begin grief counseling about two weeks after Todd's passing and decided to stay with Dr. Terry, our marriage counselor. I had no expectations. I knew there were no words that could possibly comfort me. I could barely muster the energy or desire to get dressed and make it to my appointment. Unlike when I first met with Dr. Terry, seeking help to save my marriage and myself, I wasn't seeking anything this time. As I walked into her office, she greeted me with a heartfelt hug. I was overcome with emotion. The last time I had seen her, Todd and I were leaving her office on a high note, happy and hopeful about our future. I stared at the spot where Todd had stood and recalled our last session together. We were at peace that day. I remembered Dr. Terry standing between us like the black-and-white-shirted referee I originally imagined, but cheering enthusiastically for *both* sides. Now, two weeks later, I was standing in her office alone. I had been there last as a wife, but now I stood there as a widow.

Dr. Terry and I didn't talk much during that first session. She allowed me to cry for nearly the entire hour. In between wiping my tears and blowing my nose, I stated how none of the issues in my marriage that had led me to her mattered any longer. I said I could barely even remember our problems. I couldn't believe I had ever felt emotionally disconnected from Todd. I forgot I hadn't liked him for a season, and he hadn't liked me either. I couldn't recall any of the arguments and stubborn actions we'd both taken to make our points. I couldn't believe there had been a time when I felt I couldn't live with him anymore. I couldn't remember how angry I became when he was trying to control me. All of that, which had been so important to me when I first met Dr. Terry, now meant nothing. I would have given *anything* to have an argument with Todd right now. I asked myself how we had gotten things so twisted in the first place. We wasted so much time, time that we would never get back.

As I sat with Dr. Terry, I couldn't find words to express how I was feeling. She kindly explained that I didn't have to have any words. She encouraged me to live in whatever moment I found myself. She told me how important it was to embrace the space I was in. If I felt like crying, I should *feel* the tears—allow them in. She said that just as a wave in the ocean comes onto the shore and then rides back into the waters, my tears would do the same.

Dr. Terry told me about the six steps of grief: shock, denial, bargaining, depression, anger, and acceptance. She told me that my healing process would involve each step, but that they wouldn't necessarily fall in any particular order. I might experience one at a time, or two or more at a time, and I should allow each experience to become a part of me. But no matter the order of the steps of grief, acceptance is always the last.

My head was pounding and my eyes were swollen as I prepared to leave her office. Dr. Terry said I was to be commended for beginning the process toward healing so quickly. She told me that many people, particularly women, do not seek grief counseling at all. Instead they immediately try to throw themselves back into their daily lives, putting healing on the back burner. Dr. Terry warned me that grief is a part of loss, and told me how important it is to grieve properly. You can grieve on the front end, the middle, or the back end; but you *will* grieve. She advised me that it was definitely healthier to grieve on the front end, because counseling teaches you how to grieve properly. I thanked her at the end of the session. I missed Todd like crazy; but I felt a sense of hope, at least for that moment.

While trying to grapple with this immense and devastating grief, I found out that daddy was really sick. It took so much mental and emotional strength to get myself together to fly to Chicago to visit him. I was so numb from Todd's death that there was no room left for me to feel any more pain or loss.

As I drove to the hospital with my mother, my mind was drawn to the memory of Todd's last visit with my dad only a few weeks prior. Todd had not seen daddy since he'd taken a turn for the worse. The tubes, machines, and my dad's extreme weight loss shook Todd. We walked into the room and Todd went straight to the head of the bed. He placed his hand on daddy's forehead and began to pray for him. I stood on the other side of the bed, and Todd looked at me. With a confident voice, he said, "Don't count God out."

Daddy then opened his eyes, and I could see his fear and his pain. He couldn't speak, he didn't know who we were, and he was afraid. I hadn't thought about it in years, but I remembered daddy being afraid to die. He believed in God, but he questioned life after death. Even though daddy had grown spiritually before Alzheimer's took control of him, I knew he hadn't made peace with death. The fear in his eyes that day haunted me. As Todd and I stood outside his room, I told him about daddy's fear. Todd assured me he would be fine.

I wanted my dad to be at peace. I went back to his room to give him a kiss before I left. As I placed my lips on his forehead, he opened his eyes again. I told him I loved him and would see him again soon. Tears streamed down his face. I wiped his tears, held his hand, and cried with him. As Todd and I prepared to leave my mom's house to return to Columbus, he promised her that we would be back in two weeks to check on her and dad. Todd never made it back. He passed away two days before our scheduled trip.

Now I was back in Chicago and daddy was in hospice care. Alzheimer's had taken its toll. He was suffering from pneumonia, and his prognosis was not good. Growing up, I had never known my father to be sick. He never had headaches; he never had a cold. He never even took time off of work due to illness. He was always busy doing something, mostly providing for his family. He was a handsome, strong, and vibrant man. *Wow, it dawned on me that these were the very same words I had used to describe my husband, Todd.* Now his life was coming to an end, and in his mind, he was alone. Even though he was breathing on his own, I knew he wouldn't survive much longer. My heart felt numb. It had only been three weeks since Todd's death, and here I was, dealing with the demons of death again.

I looked at my mom and wondered how could she continue to survive through so many losses. She lost her only sister, her grandson Rodney, who died of a brain hemorrhage when he was twenty-six years old, two daughters, her mother, and her son-in law. She even survived breast cancer. And now she stood next to her husband as he lay dying. I couldn't fathom her strength. I returned home. A few days later James called and suggested I come back because daddy was not going to make it much longer. But I couldn't do it. I didn't go.

⬿

The day daddy passed away, my mom, Marie, James, Keith, and Kenneth were at his side. I sat at home on the phone with Marie who told me when daddy stopped breathing. I asked if mom was okay, and she said "yes." I hung up the phone and sat for more than an hour, pondering on how fragile life is. I reflected upon my childhood struggles with my dad. I relived the good times we'd shared, and I remembered how strong, handsome, and determined he was. I remembered his working two and three jobs to take care of us while never complaining. I remembered his retirement party after forty-six years with E. J. Brach and Sons, which was the largest retirement party the company had ever thrown. That was the first time I ever danced with my father. Daddy's hard work, dedication, and accomplishments were even recognized by the then Mayor of Chicago, Harold Washington.

I wondered if the fear of dying lost its hold on daddy before he passed. I hoped he was finally at peace. Then my thoughts were drawn back to Todd. He had passed away twenty-eight days earlier, and now my dad was gone too. I laughed as I thought how surprised daddy would be to see Todd in heaven.

The funeral services of both my father and Todd still run together in my mind. Sometimes I can't separate them. The two most important men in my life were gone. I felt completely alone. I was finding it unbearable to be at my house. The silence was overwhelming, and I could feel Todd's presence in every corner. I could even smell him. Everything in our home spoke his name. There were times I instinctively reached for my phone to call him to see if he wanted to meet for lunch, or to share something with him about my day. I was in a dazed stupor most of the time. The nights were even worse. When everything was dark and quiet around two in the morning, I was alone with my thoughts. And the most devastating of all was waking up in the middle of the night and realizing there was no one on the other side of my bed.

I could have gone home to Chicago to escape the loneliness, but I knew my family would smother me with attention, which wasn't what I needed. Then one day my girlfriend, Nikol, whose husband, William, had played in the NFL with Todd, suggested I come and stay with her and her family for as long as I needed. My heart was touched and I was relieved. I knew Nikol would give me the space I needed. She and Edie had already been the perfect help for me: they knew when to keep their distance, and they knew when to get close enough to hold me up. Nikol, William, and their children were wonderful. Her mom, dad, grandparents, and sisters whom I had never met before, all embraced me as one of their own. They made sure I had plenty of food, made it to my appointments, and got my rest. When Nikol wasn't with me, Edie was with me. Edie has a silent strength that still holds me up today.

I continued seeing both my therapist and my regular physician, Dr. Sharkis, every week. My doctor checked my blood pressure and asked me questions about my sleeping patterns, my anxiety levels, and my diet. I was beginning to show signs of depression, so he suggested I consider taking something. But I refused to take any medication. I figured my grief counseling sessions would be enough. As time passed, I became more withdrawn and unable to rest. I had no appetite, I was very angry, and I developed a terrible "whatever" attitude. As the weeks passed and I became more and more distraught, I wanted to lash out. I wanted someone to be held accountable for Todd's death. But the only thing I could blame was his genetics.

Todd had done everything he knew to ensure he had a long life. He didn't smoke, do drugs, drink, or eat unhealthy foods, and he exercised six days a week. Even when we were on vacation, Todd had a workout bag with him. And even though he had a physical every year, his heart disease went undetected. Three weeks prior to his death, there were no signs that he was ill. If there had been some signs, perhaps we could have prevented this.

Why were there no signs? I just couldn't understand. The lesser I understood, the angrier I became. And I began directing my anger toward God. I didn't blame God for Todd's death, but I couldn't understand why He allowed it. I was so angry because I didn't get to say goodbye.

I was raised to believe that everything happens for a reason and that there are no coincidences in life. Todd's death changed so much for me. My faith was tested like never before. When my aunt, Denise, Delores, my mom and my dad became ill, I prayed to God for their healing and for the strength of our family. But I couldn't pray for Todd because he left so suddenly, and I had no strength to pray for myself.

My days and nights became one. God, the one source I knew that could mend my hurting heart, was the one to whom I tied Todd's death. Todd lived a life dedicated to God, and God had let him down. I asked God over and over again, "Why now? And why like this?" I knew there were people praying for me, but I refused to go to God myself. I did something I never thought I would even consider: I turned my back on God. I stopped praying, studying, and trusting. I knew who God was, but I didn't want to be in His presence. I was hurting, and I wanted him to know it. *As if He didn't.* I ignored Him. I wouldn't speak His name.

⁓⁂⁓

Because I continued to refuse to take sleeping pills or antidepressants, my doctor suggested I drink six ounces of red wine before going to bed. That took the edge off, and allowed me to sleep more than a few hours at a time. Then I got the idea that a little more wine would make me feel even better. So I began to drink eight ounces a night, and then ten.

One night I was hurting so badly I drank an entire bottle. As I lay down on the sofa, my head was spinning and I felt very ill. I had the worst headache. I couldn't move. About an hour later, I had no choice—I just made it to the bathroom before the wine and food forced its way out of me. I dragged myself to my bed and vowed to never drink like that again. I awoke the following morning with a pounding headache, a stark reminder of the vow I made the night before. I decided that drinking was not the answer.

I became so unfeeling that even my therapist suggested antidepressants. When I told her I didn't want to be this way—not to mention I also didn't care about coming out of it—she asked me very gingerly if I ever had thoughts of suicide. I assured her that although I was in a very dark place, suicide never crossed my mind. I finally realized I needed something to pull me out of this deep, dark hole, and therefore I agreed to try the medication.

My doctor gave me a prescription for antidepressants and sleeping pills. After a few days, I began to take both. The antidepressants really did suppress my emotions. I was rested and very mellow. I didn't feel anything, and it was wonderful. The medicine helped me cope with my loss and work through grief counseling as I fought to understand my new normal. I had been trying to deal with the shock of Todd's death, but I'd fallen into depression and anger simultaneously. And thus, I couldn't make my way to the other stages of grief. I was so angry about him not coming back and I continued to take this anger out on God.

In church, I listened as Pastor Tillman taught about the love and mercy of God. I listened as he described God's faithfulness and saving grace. But the more I listened, the angrier I became. I wondered: *Where was God's saving grace and faithfulness when Todd needed Him? Where was God's mercy when Todd suffered a heart attack?* I was screaming inside my head for answers. I was hurt and disappointed. The more Pastor Tillman preached, the more distance I felt between God and me. I had no hope, I had no peace, and I felt no joy or contentment. All I felt was loneliness and grief. I didn't allow myself to feel the love of God because I didn't want to. My pain was so intense I did not know if I could survive it. I pulled further and further away from God—or at least I thought I did.

After about eight months of antidepressants and sleeping pills, the medication stopped working. My doctor recommended a few additional options, but I told him I didn't want to take any more drugs. He said I would need to be weaned off the antidepressant; so he lowered my dose, which enabled the start of the weaning process. It was awful. I had no idea how dependent I had become on the antidepressants. I experienced withdrawals that left me ill. I couldn't sleep. I would lie on the floor for hours, shaking. I was hot for one minute and then cold the next. I became disoriented and my depression grew worse.

I was only taking a very small amount of the antidepressant when I decided that being weaned off was not working for me. I stopped taking them completely to allow my body to rid itself of the toxins the drug caused. To say it was the worst physical experience I've ever endured is putting it mildly. I am not speaking negatively about antidepressants because they were a temporary fix; but I knew that nothing would ease me until I released the pain of Todd's death to God. By this point I didn't even recognize myself. I had thoughts and behavioral patterns that were not Daphne. The medication and the stress were causing my hair to fall out. Ironically, chemotherapy would not be the cause of *this* hair loss, as I once had feared throughout the course of my entire life. I had terrible hives and swelling on my face and lips. I assumed I had developed an allergic reaction to something, but my dermatologist couldn't find any cause. I returned to my regular doctor. He told me that my body was reacting to all the stress and trauma it was going through.

I experienced some of my most uncomfortable moments when people expressed their condolences. While I knew they meant well, some of their comments were crushing.

"Be strong."

"He's in a better place now."

"Todd's debt was paid. It was his time."

"Even if Todd could come back, he wouldn't."

I don't recall who said that to me, but when I was told Todd wouldn't come back even if he could, I asked, "How do you know Todd wouldn't come back?" I found no comfort in the idea that Todd's debt was paid. His debt was not paid to *me*; he still owed me some things. He owed me time, he owed me love, and I want to collect on all of it.

I knew I shouldn't have responded so negatively when people attempted to console me. I knew I needed them. I knew I needed their presence to draw strength from. I needed their shoulders to cry on. I needed their ears to listen. I needed their prayers. But I didn't need words, at least not right away. Edie, Nikol, Mel, and Margaret listened as I talked about Todd repeatedly. They cried with me and held me up. They followed my lead, and they were just what I needed them to be. Some of Todd's former NFL teammates and colleagues also reached out to me, including Ronnie Lott, Willie Gault, Shaun Gayle, Leslie Frazier, Eric Allen, and Keith Byars. They phoned every so often to make sure I was holding up. They were always respectful and compassionate, while offering their assistance if I needed anything. I will always appreciate their displays of compassion.

I was anxious to feel better and to get back to living; but I felt as if I was buried under bricks of pain and sadness. My mind and my spirit were out of sync. In my mind I wanted out of the dark place, but my spirit was so wounded and low that I didn't posses enough strength, passion, or faith to push my way out. My depression grew and my strength weakened. I was warring between my flesh and my spirit. These were the days when I didn't see the truth of God's Word. My flesh was angry and my spirit was hurt. So the Word of God became nothing more than just a book. I lost my connection to the spirit of the Word. My faith was in need of major repair. I was sure that I would live the rest of my life in this way—filled with pain, disappointment, grief, guilt, lack of motivation, lack of faith, and lack of passion. Thankfully, I was wrong. God delivered me when He felt it was time for me to come out of that dark place.

One afternoon, after I returned home from Dr. Terry's office, I was going through Todd's closet when I came across a notebook. It was full of lists that were written by Todd. He had columns entitled "My weaknesses," "My strengths," "My improvements," and "Improvements needed." The date was January 2005, two months before he passed. My heart sank as I read Todd's acknowledgements from his own perspective. He listed "not being emotionally available" and "not communicating well" as weaknesses, and "caring" and "listening well" as strengths. In the "Improvements needed" column, he'd written that he needed to trust himself enough to communicate with me more freely. In the "Improvements" column, he'd written that he knew he could trust me.

There were pages and pages of this. I sobbed until there were no more tears. As I pulled myself up, I stopped and stared at Todd's suits, shirts, ties, sweaters, slacks, and shoes. I looked around his closet and I could smell him so strongly. The oils and cologne he wore were still in his clothing. I stood there gazing at how neatly Todd had arranged his closet. His suits were color-coordinated, and his shirts were starched and hanging neatly on the padded hangers. His jeans and sweaters were folded on shelves. Todd had a huge tie rack, and his ties were color-coordinated as well.

The longer I stood, the weaker I became. I remember collapsing onto his suits as I screamed out his name, asking him to help me understand what happened. I suddenly became angry with Todd. I grabbed his suits and shirts and began throwing them out of the closet and onto the bedroom floor.

"How could you take such good care of everything in your life and not know you were sick?!" I screamed.

I was so overcome with pain; I began to feel faint. I could not control my tears or my anger. For a moment I thought to call Edie to come and rescue me because I knew I was losing it. But I couldn't do it. With all of Todd's clothing on the floor in the middle of our bedroom, I turned off the closet light, walked over to our bed, and fell onto it.

I lay on the bed and felt as if I were sinking, not physically sinking into the mattress, but as if my spirit were sinking into a very dark place. I remember wondering: *Is this what it feels like to die?* As I lay there I did not fight being pulled down. The more I felt I was being pulled, the darker the space became. I did not resist, nor did I fight back. I didn't want to die; however I lacked the strength to save myself. I fell into the darkest place in my soul.

I wanted to go to sleep because I didn't want to feel the pain anymore. I couldn't go to sleep and I knew I wasn't dreaming. But then, something inside of me lifted wherein it didn't feel so dark for that moment. My mind's eye looked up and above me was a very small light. I was not overcome by the light; it did not get bigger or brighter. And throughout all of this my physical eyes remained shut. *Is this a spiritual experience?*

I continued to lie there and I distinctly remember thinking, *whatever*. As my spirit grew closer to this light, I began to weep. And at that moment, my spirit finally found its way out of the darkness. I realized I was still alive, and I wept harder. For the first time since Todd passed, I cried out to God to help me. I asked God to show me where to put my pain. I told God that if I continued to live like this I would physically die . . . indeed the pain was killing me.

Suddenly I heard the words: *You will do what Todd would do; you will give back.* I didn't know at the time what that meant, but I would soon learn the good that would result from Todd's death. God would trade my pain for passion. God never allows us to endure more than we can handle. Right at this moment, I began to think of my mother, and her immense strength throughout my life. I thought of her spending most of her days in the kitchen, preparing home-cooked meals for her family, taking only short breaks and never complaining. I thought of her taking care of Delores and Denise, and the strength it took for her to watch her children die yet still go on. Then I thought of her fighting for her own life. When she was diagnosed with breast cancer, my mom rolled up her emotional sleeves and got ready for the fight of her life. And she *fought*. She never complained about her cancer and never asked, *why me?* After my mom's surgery, she told me that God had far exceeded her prayers, and that she had nothing to complain about. My mother didn't talk about her strength—she *lived* her strength. I knew that the pull of my mother's strength was what I needed the most.

Several days later, my friends, Margaret Bell and BeBe Winans who are professional gospel singers, invited me to join them in Los Angeles, California, where BeBe was hosting a concert. I knew it would do me much good to get away for a little while, so I happily agreed to go. At one point during the concert, BeBe began singing about God's forgiveness. The song was beautiful, but the word *forgiveness* grabbed my heart and would not let go. I kept hearing *forgiveness, forgiveness.*

All of a sudden I knew it was time to ask God to forgive me for neglecting my relationship with Him. So I raised my hands and asked to be forgiven. I told God I forgave Him too. I had to forgive God before I could go on. I forgave God for allowing Todd to die. I forgave God for allowing Todd to die alone behind the steering wheel of his vehicle. I forgave God for not allowing us to realize that Todd was sick. I forgave God for not allowing me the opportunity to say goodbye to Todd. I forgave God for not allowing Todd and I to grow old together. I even forgave God for our never having children.

The great thing about God is that He knew my feelings toward Him; but more importantly, He knew my heart. He knew I needed to be forgiven, and even though He never needs forgiveness, God knew I needed to forgive Him for myself. I gave up judging God and embraced His love again. As I forgave God, because of His loving kindness and mercy, God forgave me.

Lastly, I forgave myself for being so angry with God. I felt connected to God again. For the first time in more than a year, I felt good about life. I knew I was on the road to a better me. I knew I was going to survive this tragedy.

⁂

We are not promised another day to get it right. If more of us really lived by that, we would not let the sun go down on our day without working out our issues with our family and friends. We don't always have more time. Tomorrow may never come.

My grieving and healing process was long and arduous. There were times when I would get through a day feeling good and upbeat about my life and myself. I thought I had made it to the other side of my pain. But then the very next day I would struggle to get out of bed or feel unable to get through the next moment. I knew, however, that it was all a part of the healing process. I gave myself time, and I was patient with myself.

I can't say that I got over my sorrow, but I did get through it. I took it one minute and one step at a time. And slowly, seconds turned into minutes, minutes into hours, hours into days, days into weeks, weeks into months, and months into years. There were times when I walked through it, there were times when I crawled through it, and there were times when I felt I would not get through another day. But the sun does shine again, and I did get to the other side of the hurt. I will never forget my losses, but their hold on me did lose its strength.

People would ask if I was better. My first thought was usually to respond, "No." But even when I didn't feel better, I was becoming different, and different eventually became my better. The beauty of the human spirit is that we all have the ability to survive and adjust, even in the most trying situations—*if* we choose to do so. I survived tragedy because I made a conscious decision to do so. Slowly I was getting out of bed, slowly I was eating more, slowly I began to smile again, and slowly I began to care about myself again.

I did not enjoy being alone, but it was important for me to conquer the fear of being alone. I forced myself to do things alone—things Todd and I used to do together. I started going to restaurants alone. Even though there were times when it was difficult, I continued to push myself to get through a meal alone. The first time I went to the movies alone was not easy. I don't even know the name of the movie or what it was about because I cried during the entire movie. Even though I was tempted to get up and leave, I forced myself to stay. Eventually, I even began to travel alone. It was a process. Your new normal does not happen overnight. It's one movie at a time, one meal at a time, and one trip at a time.

Now I awake everyday with a purpose. I'm in such a good place in my life today. I know I am open to receive whatever God has in store for me. I have grown by leaps and bounds while alone these past few years. I've been rediscovering myself and making the changes in my life that I need to make. I can finally say that I am at peace and that I am content. I am becoming the Daphne I was born to be. I am happy with me. Self-love and self-acceptance are rewarding experiences.

A PICTORIAL JOURNAL

MY JOURNEY CONTINUES

LEFT Todd loving the game of football.

RIGHT Todd being so focused on his opponent.

LEFT Todd moving with such speed.

ABOVE We are husband and wife as we head to our reception.

LEFT Mom and dad on my wedding day.

RIGHT Keith and Kenneth on my wedding day.

LEFT Todd's Chicago Bears teammate and groomsmen, Mike Singletary and Shaun Gayle.

RIGHT Daddy delivers speech at his retirement party from Brach.

LEFT Mom and dad dancing at his retirement party. I've always loved seeing them on the dance floor.

RIGHT Daddy and his twin sister, Lois, at his retirement party. Her presence is our surprise gift to him. He is shocked.

LEFT Our Aruba trip. Todd loves being in and near the water.

BELOW On our way to snorkel with friends in Aruba.

RIGHT Todd regrets our return to the States after our vacation in Aruba.

LEFT Beneath the chilly waters of Dunn's River Falls, Jamaica.

RIGHT Todd's high school class reunion.

ABOVE Denise being her beautiful self.

ABOVE Todd and Anika after she pays an awesome tribute to him during her graduation dinner.

LEFT My dad's biological father. I'm 33 years old when I see this photo. This is when I first discover the family secret.

RIGHT Daddy is so handsome.

TODD'S DAILY ROUTINE

ABOVE Exercising

ABOVE Mentoring young people.

LEFT Motivating young people.

RIGHT Working in ministry.

ABOVE My parent's 50th wedding anniversary.

ABOVE My parents upon renewing their wedding vows.

LEFT Marie enjoys two of her favorite things: food and laughter.

RIGHT Mom's 80th birthday party. She's a survivor.

LEFT I'm reporting the news at the Radio One studio.

RIGHT My morning show co-host, Paul Strong; the prankster.

LEFT I'm just *chilling* after the morning show. I need to go to my office.

ABOVE My pastor and first lady, Bishop Howard and Glenneth Tillman, *bringing lives into focus with the Word.* They continue to stand with me.

ABOVE My friend, Nikol and me. She keeps me laughing.

ABOVE *Where's Daphne?* Edie is my mother hen. Can't you see it in her eyes?

RIGHT Anika and me at the Indiana Black Expo 2010. Our relationship is so wonderful now!

LEFT So excited! My girlfriend, Margaret, and I arrive in South Africa with BeBe and CeCe Winans for the AIDS awareness tour.

RIGHT BeBe and I are waiting for our luggage at the airport in South Africa. I can't wait to get to our hotel.

ABOVE Pastor Howard Tillman, Todd's boss, Mac Stewart, Ph.D., me, and Todd's brother, Archie, Ohio State University unveils the Todd Bell Resource Center.

ABOVE I'm sharing words of appreciation at the Todd Bell Luncheon.

ABOVE My champion, Dr. Thomas Ryan. I appreciate his support and kindness.

ABOVE My *go-to* friend, William White, Columbus Mayor Michael Coleman, me, Archie Griffin, Provost Joe Alutto, and Mac Stewart, Ph.D. at the Todd Bell lecture series fundraiser.

RIGHT My hero, Dr. Quinn Capers (I love this guy). and my dear friend, Keith Byars.

LEFT Todd and his youngest brother, Sean (left). Todd loved his baby brother.

LEFT Todd's Team walkers stretch before the Walk.

BELOW A portion of Todd's Team.

RIGHT Todd's Team joins the Columbus American Heart Association Walk.

LEFT A night out in Washington, D.C., with my brother, James.

RIGHT My favorite photo of Todd and me. I miss having him to lean on.

BELOW And this is who we are . . . still standing—my siblings and me.

18

WHAT I KNOW NOW

I know now that I have always been a survivor. I survived my dad's lack of an emotional connection with me. I survived his strong hand of discipline, but fell prey to his weak hand of showing love. I survived the abuse of my first marriage. I survived the breakdown of my second marriage. I survived the loss of my sisters, my dad, and my husband. I escaped all the pain in my life by becoming a survivor, but I know now that survival alone is not enough. Survival can never take the place of self-love or the love from another.

I know now that my desire to please others robbed me of my desire to please myself. I didn't know what I wanted for *me*. I believed that if I pleased others, I would be pleased. I believed that if I could get other people to like me, then I would feel love . . . the love I never experienced from my father.

You don't get to pick your family, but you can choose the role you will play within your family. I appreciate the family I've been given. My mom, dad, and siblings are a part of who I am. My experiences with my father taught me not to allow fear to guide me emotionally and thus close my heart to the possibility of love. My mom's love gave me strength and courage. Delores' love taught me to give life all you have and know that no matter how bad things are today, tomorrow will be better. Denise's love taught me to never ignore the negative issues in my life, to let go of pride, and to ask for forgiveness. Todd's love taught me that love is action, love is work, love is forever, and life is fragile. I learned from Todd that even though we leave this earth because of the love we leave behind, we live forever!

My marriage was a great challenge at times. When things were good, they were really good; but when they were bad, they were really bad. My marriage to Todd was the most work I had ever put into anything. We made our share of mistakes. There were days I felt no love at all. But through all of it, I enjoyed being married and I enjoyed being Todd's wife. I wanted to meet his expectations. Mind you, I don't view this as being weak. I wasn't a perfect wife, nor was Todd a perfect husband; but we were on our way to becoming perfect for each other. I miss being accountable to him.

The pain of losing Todd caused my heart and soul to shut down. I could not see past the moment, and I could not see myself on the other side of my pain. Eventually, God's love lifted me and carried me to the other side of my grief. I still think of Todd every day, and I probably always will. Each day I continue to heal, but there are times when I still live in my yesterday. I still long for one more moment with Todd. I still ask myself if I missed something that could have saved his life.

I know now that Todd could not make me happy, although I expected him to. I depended on him for my happiness, and that was not his responsibility. I put too much pressure on Todd, expecting him to complete me. I know now that he couldn't. His role was to complement me, and my role was to complement him. My anger toward Todd was not because he didn't love me; it was because I didn't love myself.

I know now that I am the only one who can make me happy. I know my happiness starts on the inside. I used to be unable to live the life I knew I deserved. Because I had not learned to love *me*, I was angry and disappointed; but I wouldn't look inside myself for the reasons. I knew that the pain would be intense if I really took the time to look into my innermost thoughts. I know now that today I am a new me, and God is allowing me to live with some normalcy. I have learned to live in the moment of my life.

I know now that choosing life is not always easy, especially if you have been wounded and broken. The easy choice is sometimes just to give in and give up. It takes no effort to just exist, but it takes hard work, passion, and motivation to live. After all the sadness I have suffered through, I finally understand that I am strong—just like my mom. I know now that just like her I can make it. I have the courage to stand and fight for my life. Even during my weakest moments after Todd's death, I know now that I was strong. I had the will to live, but it was buried beneath my pain. Regaining and recreating my life was difficult work. I had to will myself to go on.

I know now that things can change in mind, body, soul, and spirit if we desire. Our difficulties may be tremendous; but if we believe, we will get past it. Circumstances will change and impossibilities will yield. Sometimes we have to take our eyes off of what our lives are and see through the eyes of faith to see what our lives can be—and what our lives are meant to be.

I know now that there is a plan for each of us. The road we travel to get there will make us who we were born to be. Now I am where I am supposed to be, doing what I was born to do. The pain in my life didn't kill me; it actually drew me to a higher calling.

I could not embrace that reality four years ago because in some strange way my pain comforted me. It hurt not to hurt. I know now that none of us is so special that our lives will be filled with all good days. I had to come to the end of myself. And when I did, God was right where He had always been—waiting for me

DAPHNE BELL

to let go of my pain and give it to Him. God's tender compassion rescued me.

Life is a privilege, not a right. We have a right to live, but we don't have a right to take our lives for granted. Life is a gift. Life is fragile and short. The next moment is not promised to us. I know that for sure. I know now that our true character is defined by the hard times—the painful moments. We won't always feel on top of the world. There will be days when we will feel like the world is on top of us. But it won't always be this way. When your day is too hard to handle, hold on. You *will* gain strength.

It's strange, but I know now that my pain and depression were really a wonderful place for me because in that place I found freedom. My faith was tested, and I proved that I had the faith to move on. Life is so much more than happiness; it is so much more than having everything go our way. I know now that even when I don't feel happy, I can always feel peace and joy—if I choose.

I know now that everything I need lies within me because God put it there: strength, courage, joy, love, forgiveness, righteousness, purpose, passion, and wisdom. I can draw from it at any time because God is always there, willing to replenish what I allow to slip away from me. Even though I felt like I was alone for many days and nights, I know now that I was never alone. God was always there. Because God is a gentleman, He did not force Himself on me. God allowed me to find my way back to Him with His loving kindness.

I know now I had to feel each and every phase of my loss in order to have a full recovery. The way you get better depends on you. Everything in life is a choice. I could have chosen to die in my pain, I could have chosen to remain withdrawn from my life, and I could have chosen to remain angry. I know now that God allowed me to be angry with Him. God allowed me to disconnect myself from Him. God allowed me to be disappointed in Him—but only for a time.

God always felt my pain. He did not rescue me because of my many pity parties. He did not lift me up because of my anger, tears, sadness, grief, and guilt. God rescued me when I believed He could and would. God rescued me when I stopped praying with my own words and began to pray His Word. My words were filled with the bitterness of death, the sorrow of the grave. But, God's Word is full of life. When I let go of my own thoughts, God met me.

I know now that the worst times in my life have introduced me to the best times of my life. The path becomes clear if you choose to see beyond your pain and disappointment. I sowed many tears throughout the years, but today I reap in joy. Things do balance out and come together. The peace of God that surpasses all understanding keeps my heart and mind in perfect peace.

Life is full of many highs and lows. I know now that we will all fall sometimes, we will all hurt, and we will all cry. But we will get back up again and experience love, joy, and freedom! Our dark days will become light!

❦

I know now that God did not allow Todd's death as a way to hurt me, disappoint me, frustrate me, or cause me pain. I know now that my challenges and experiences were really not all about me. It was all to line me up with my purpose and my reason for being born.

The pain didn't kill me because out of my pain, this story is told. God traded my pain for passion—a passion to share my story, with the hope that you will gain something from my experiences. Writing this book is not about the work and pain it took to do so; it's about its purpose. I know now that this assignment, which was given to me through encouragement and love, is meant for you. Reaching back into my past was not easy. Some things I didn't want to remember. Some things I didn't want to share. My life, thoughts, choices, and mistakes were the source of my pain; but through God, I found the strength to push my inner fears out of my way and trust that all would be well. As

I sat writing these words, many days I could not hold back the tears.

I know now that I live in a new normal; but more importantly, I LIVE! I know now that I am present in my life again, and in many ways present in my life for the first time. I know now that God loves me, cares for me, wants the best for me, and is able to provide *the best* better than I could ever provide. His love changes me day by day. I have learned how to live loved. I now know me—a woman of God, loved by God, who lives because of God.

There has been a lot of pain in my life, and the pain didn't kill me not because it couldn't kill me, but because I made the decision to choose life in the midst of my pain. My pain broke me and it wounded me, but it also made me strong. Even when I was sure I could go no further, my pain pushed me into another place in my life. With each challenge and with each loss, the pain and the recovery made me who I am today. I know now that I am stronger and wiser because of my pain.

I know now that weeping endures for the night, but joy does come in the morning. Isn't it amazing that the pain didn't kill me?

Indeed we count them blessed who endure. You have heard of the perservance of Job and seen the end intended by the Lord—that the Lord is very compassionate and merciful.

James 5:11

Now the LORD blessed the latter days of Job more than his beginning...

Job 42:12

In Heartfelt Memory of My Mother

On January 9th, 2010, my mother, Agnes Cunningham, lost her sixteen-year battle with breast cancer. Though she understood that her body could not fight any longer, she hoped against all hope to be here to see the release of this book. My mom fully supported and encouraged me in all of my endeavors, and she was very proud of me for telling my story with the intent to change and to save lives. She was also very excited to have her name in print, which brought me so much joy as she allowed me to interview her and challenge her to reach into her past and bring substance to this book. My mom was the one constant in my life; and although I miss her more than words can describe, I still feel her with me every day. Her style, her love, and her strength made me who I am today. God knew it was time for her to take her rest and He received her back to Himself. Although she is no longer here in the natural, her spirit is still very much alive and present— and I believe she knows my purpose.

Good night mom, I'll see you in the morning.

EPILOGUE

Keeping Tabs on Your Heart

Todd was a man who led by example. He was a mentor and a teacher. If Todd saw a need, and if it was within his power to help, without hesitation he would lend his support. He was a true giver; he believed in paying it forward, a valuable philosophy he learned from his OSU football coach, Woody Hayes. Todd's giving spirit continues even after his death: The work I now do in his memory is, in large part, because I did not want Todd's death to be in vain.

After Todd passed, I began learning all I could about heart disease, the "silent killer" that is claiming so many lives unnecessarily. God traded my pain for this passion. I started a nonprofit organization called Keeping TABs on Your Heart (T.A.B. is for Todd Anthony Bell), which helps people research the medical history of their families, identify red flags related to chronic disease, initiate healthy lifestyles (like increased physical activity and proper nutrition), and effectively manage their current health issues. My campaign aims to educate families and to promote healthy lifestyle management in order to prevent chronic heart diseases. If you'd like to learn more about what we do, you can find us online at www.ktoyh.org.

Jeff Wilson, the general manager of Radio One Columbus, supports my passion for creating awareness about heart disease. He's given me the opportunity to do a segment on three Radio One stations, called "Keeping TABs on Your Heart with Daphne Bell." I partner with the OSU Medical Center staff and physicians to continue educating people and spreading the word about this epidemic. As the host of the show, I talk to doctors and other health care professionals, discussing topics ranging from hypertension to diabetes, cholesterol, stress, diet, exercise, and family history, and how it all relates to heart disease.

The topics chosen for the program are a collaborative effort between Toni Hare, Director of Communications at the Ross Heart Hospital, and me. After the subject matter is decided, I begin my research, and Toni assigns the appropriate physician or health care professional to present the health-related issues to our listening audience. I am very fortunate to have such a wonderful team; they completely get it. Even though they are highly trained in their fields of expertise, they converse on the air as if they are casually sharing information with a friend. It makes my job that much easier, and the impact of their personalities is well received in the community.

If one life is saved or changed because of my tragedy, I can end my day feeling fulfilled. And I know I will have another opportunity to reach another person tomorrow.

With the support of the Richard M. Ross Heart Hospital and the Columbus American Heart Association, I also formed Todd's Team. Walkers participate in the annual American Heart Association Walk each summer by making a financial contribution to help raise funds for heart disease research. We walk in memory of Todd, along with at least forty thousand other people, for one cause: to end this silent killer.

When I first began my campaign, I didn't feel as if the church community would embrace my purpose. But it turns out that my pastor and his wife, Bishop Howard and Glenneth Tillman, have been my biggest supporters, encouraging and motivating me to share my story to help save lives. Pastors throughout the state of Ohio and their congregations have all embraced my ministry and continue to support my mission.

The work I do on heart disease prevention is only a small part of Todd's legacy. After Todd left the NFL, he began scheduling regular "rap sessions" with African-American men on the OSU campus to encourage them to pursue their dreams by completing their education. Todd also began a mentoring and tutoring program on campus. He reached out to young men in high school to encourage them to consider furthering their education by attending OSU. If he learned someone was contemplating not attending or dropping out of college, Todd would personally reach out to the individual. Under his watch, Ohio State University initiated a Black Male Initiative to rectify the dismal graduation rates.

In honor of Todd's heartfelt work, OSU created the Todd Anthony Bell National Resource Center for the African-American Male. Now African-American men have a place to go for support, encouragement, advice, tutoring, and fellowship as they prepare for their futures. Almost two-thirds of the African-American men in college are not graduating. However, the graduation rate for the African-American men at OSU increased from 47 to 57 percent in 2008. The Bell Resource Center has had a significant impact on these statistics. OSU's first-year retention rate for African-American males is now at 91 percent, which is close to the university average of 93 percent.

In addition, OSU hosts an annual Todd A. Bell Lecture Series fundraising luncheon, which has featured sports legends and keynote speakers such as: Archie Griffin, Clark Kellogg, Keith Byars, Cris Carter, OSU Athletic Director Gene Smith, and OSU Head Football Coach Jim Tressel. To learn more about the Bell Resource Center, go to: www.oma.osu.edu/brc.

The outpouring of gratitude for Todd continues. His hometown, Middletown, Ohio, paid tribute to his memory in a very special way. In 2006, the city council voted to name a street in his memory, Todd Bell Memorial Way. The vote had the full support of the city's mayor and all members of the city council. Two years later, on September 19, 2008, the city of Middletown hosted an event to reveal the street name to the community, which I attended. When I saw the street sign for the first time, I was so touched. My heart was filled with gratitude that Todd's name would live forever in the place where he grew up, gave back, and learned to be an athlete and a man.

If there is a way to know what's happening on earth after we pass on, I hope Todd knows how much he was loved and appreciated.

RESOURCE GUIDE

Because Todd didn't know that which could have saved his life, I speak for him. Had Todd survived his disease, I know he would have carried the same message I do—know your family history; it can save your life.

Todd did not smoke, drink, or do drugs. He stayed away from caffeine, and 99 percent of the time he didn't eat pork, beef, or junk food. Todd worked out six days a week. I have never known a man more disciplined than Todd. He was totally committed to health and wellness. He did everything he knew to ensure longevity. At the age of forty-six, Todd still looked as good as he did during his playing days in the NFL.

I thought Todd would be here forever. I never worried about what would happen to me if my own health failed; I had Todd and I knew he would always be there for me.

During our last Friday night dinner together, I said to him, "You're going to live forever aren't you?"

He responded: "I plan to get as close to it as possible."

Yet Todd succumbed to triple coronary heart disease at the age of forty-six. He died suddenly: no warning, no symptoms, and no indication that he was sick. At his last physical, only three weeks prior to his death, his blood work came back fine, his blood pressure was excellent, his triglycerides were normal, his total cholesterol was normal, and his bad cholesterol was only slightly elevated.

How was Todd's disease missed? We didn't know his family history. Heart disease is the number 1 killer in America, and it can catch people completely without warning. For some, like Todd, the first symptom is death.

Heart disease has no respect for people. Heart disease did not care that Todd was a husband, son, brother, uncle, godparent, friend, mentor, business partner, and Christian. Heart disease does not consider your income, the neighborhood you live in, or the influence you have in your community, at your church, or on your job. We must respect this disease by being informed enough to keep it out of our lives and the lives of our loved ones. Knowledge is power—and in this case, knowledge can save your life.

The single most important weapon we have against heart disease is knowing our family history. Todd didn't know his, and I didn't learn of it until after he passed, but his mother's father died of heart disease, and his mother's brother died on the operating table during open-heart surgery. Like so many of us, Todd didn't understand the value of his past. He didn't know he was genetically predisposed to heart disease. That lack of knowledge cost him his life.

After Todd's death, I hired a specialist to read his autopsy report. He told me if we had known Todd had heart disease, he could have gone through a procedure that would have saved his life. The autopsy report showed that Todd's disease began when he was around nine years old. The report also showed that Todd was born with a defective heart. It revealed major blockage in his arteries. His arteries were 85, 90, and 95 percent blocked. They were so impacted and hard that the blood supply to his heart could no longer get past the blockage. Here was a man who played sports in high school, college, and in the NFL!

My friend, Dr. Quinn Capers, a cardiologist at the Richard M. Ross Heart Hospital in Columbus, Ohio, helped me put things in perspective. He reassured me that Todd's extremely healthy lifestyle *did* extend his life. Based on the findings from the autopsy, Dr. Capers believed that Todd probably would have died ten years earlier if his lifestyle had been anything other than what it was.

⁓

The consequences of not knowing your family's heredity health issues could be staggering. But because some families don't typically discuss medical history, many of us are not aware that we are pre-disposed to cancer, diabetes, hypertension, heart disease, and so on. Not all disease starts with you.

So many of us don't want to know. But let me help you get over that right now: in some cases, what you don't know can kill you. It is better to go to the doctor to find out what's wrong rather than to not go; it is better than having the doctor explain to your family the cause of your death.

So what don't you know that you should know? You have to shake your family tree. It is no longer acceptable to think that your grandparents died of old age. No one dies of old age. We all die of something. What did your family members die of? Do you know if your parents or grandparents have high blood pressure? Does anyone in your family have high cholesterol or diabetes? Does anyone in your family suffer from depression, alcoholism, or mental illness? Is anyone in your family living with heart disease or cancer?

It's time to acknowledge what's going on in the lives of our families. I understand we don't like to sit around the dinner table and discuss what Uncle George, Aunt Sally, and Grandma died of. It's uncomfortable to discuss sickness and death. Unfortunately, sickness and death are a part of life. And we must face them head on. If we are going to save our lives, along with the lives of our children and grandchildren, we must become proactive about our health. It's time to talk, it's time to research, and it's time to ask questions.

It's time to arm ourselves with information, and to share that information with our doctors. Our physicians are not mind readers; they only know what we tell them. Knowing your family history can change the nature of your medical procedures. Because of the strong history of breast cancer in my family, the women in my family undergo totally different screenings than women whose families do not have this history. My sister and nieces are monitored differently because of the knowledge they share with their doctors. We must become more than our doctor's patient; we must become our doctor's partner. We must not be afraid to ask questions of our doctors. We must take proactive roles in our own medical treatments.

Ask questions, demand treatment, and don't allow yourself to be dismissed until you are satisfied that your health needs have been addressed. If you are not comfortable talking to your doctor, or if your doctor does not make you feel like you are his or her highest priority, find another physician. We must know we are in a caring relationship with our physicians. Anything less is unacceptable. There are some wonderful doctors out there. Find the one who works best for you.

❦

Several studies have been published recently documenting the fact that African Americans with heart attack symptoms are less likely to be treated with state-of-the-art, lifesaving, and cardiovascular procedures than are white patients. Specifically, many studies have shown that African Americans with the same heart conditions as whites—conditions such as heart attack, congestive heart failure, and even cardiac arrest—are much less likely than whites to receive cardiac catheterization, coronary stints, open-heart surgery, pacemakers, and implanted defibrillators. Is this because of the system? Or is it because we are not aggressive enough about our health?

If you have already decided that you are not going to the doctor because of fear or because you don't think it's important, think about your family and friends. If you won't do it for yourself, do it for them. They need you. Who will take care of your parents if you are not here? Who will love and nurture your children?

More American men and women die each year from heart disease than any other form of death, including homicide. Many of these deaths are unnecessary, premature, and completely preventable. You can't just trust how you feel and look. If you approach your health with a strong passion, you will be surprised at how empowered and in charge you will feel. You may begin to treat yourself better as you get to know your body better. When you know better, you do better.

Our history speaks to us, but it doesn't have to speak *for* us. We can stop the generational curse of sickness and disease in our families by changing our thinking, our diet, and our lifestyles. Some sicknesses and diseases are random, and some are a result of where we come from. Even if you are genetically predisposed to a disease, in some cases it can be prevented and controlled, but only if you take charge of your health by first discovering your past.

When I address a group of women, I ask them what do they believe to be the number 1 threat to their health. The majority responds with "breast cancer." While breast cancer should be a concern for all of us, it is not the number 1 health threat. It is heart disease. Approximately 41,000 women die each year of breast cancer; 185,000 women die each year of heart disease. If you have hypertension, high cholesterol, or diabetes, you are at risk of developing heart disease. Talk to your doctor about further testing to ensure that you maintain a healthy heart. Tracing the illnesses suffered by your parents, grandparents, and other blood relatives can help your physician identify your risk factors and take action to keep you healthy.

Most women are the caretakers of their families. We make sure our husbands get to their doctors' appointments on time; if our children feel ill, we waste no time getting them to the hospital. But we usually do not take time off work if we are sick. We save our sick days for our family. Some women actually feel it would be selfish of them to put their own needs ahead of their families. Many of us watched our mothers live this way. But even though our intentions are good, we do our families and ourselves a disservice when we ignore our own needs. We can only give out what we have on the inside. If we are exhausted and not feeling well, our families are not getting the best of us. It is not selfish to put us first; it's actually a very selfless act. The better you feel, the healthier your family will be: mentally, physically, emotionally, and spiritually. Take some time for yourself. You are the most important person in your life.

Doctors Answer Questions About Heart Disease

I sat down with two of my champion physicians, Dr. Quinn Capers and Dr. Thomas Ryan, and asked them a few questions about heart disease. These are the same questions and answers that we have shared with our audience during my radio segment: "Keeping TABs on Your Heart with Daphne Bell."

1. WHAT IS HYPERTENSION?

Dr. Capers: Hypertension is the medical term for what we commonly call "high blood pressure." It is an extremely common disorder. When the heart contracts, it pushes blood through all of the arteries in the body. The blood inside the arteries exerts a pressure against the lining of the walls of the arteries. When this pressure is higher than normal, it promotes the buildup of atherosclerotic plaque in the arteries, which increases your risk of a heart attack, stroke, or the rupture of an aneurysm (a ballooned-out weak spot in the artery that may burst).

2. WHAT IS DIABETES?

Dr. Capers: Diabetes is a disease in which your body does not process blood sugar normally. Blood sugar is the fuel that makes your body go from your muscles to your major internal organs. In patients with diabetes, there is a problem getting the sugar from the bloodstream into the muscles and other organs, where it is needed. The blood sugar remains in the bloodstream, causing high concentrations of sugar in the blood. Although the elevated sugar can cause some serious health problems, diabetes is also associated with some non-sugar-related metabolic defects and vascular problems. Years of untreated or inadequately treated diabetes can be attributed to heart attacks, strokes, kidney failure, blindness, and poor circulation in the legs, which can result in amputation.

3. WHAT IS HIGH CHOLESTEROL?

Dr. Capers: High cholesterol means that the cholesterol in your bloodstream is at a higher-than-normal level. This could either be due to a high intake of cholesterol in your diet, or due to your body producing too much (the liver normally produces cholesterol), or a combination of the two. Over years, high cholesterol levels can cause heart attacks and strokes, due to clogged arteries.

4. IF I AM GENETICALLY PREDISPOSED TO HEART DISEASE, HYPERTENSION, DIABETES, CHOLESTEROL, AND SO ON, CAN THEY STILL BE PREVENTED?

Dr. Ryan: Heart disease can absolutely be prevented. Although genetic factors are important, and we have no control over these, lifestyle choices are just as critical to either increase or decrease the likelihood that we will someday develop heart disease. Getting regular exercise, not smoking, and following healthy diets are the most important things we can do. Developing good habits such as these early in life is important, so we should encourage our children to do so as well. Getting an adequate amount of sleep and using stress-management techniques can also be beneficial.

In addition, all adults should be screened for the risk factors discussed above. This includes tests for blood pressure, blood glucose (or sugar), lipids, and cholesterol level. These are simple tests that can help identify the major risk factors for which treatments are available. Getting these tests done regularly should be a priority for all adults, healthy or otherwise. If abnormalities are detected, talk to your physician about the choices for treatment, and make a plan that you can follow long-term to ensure that each risk factor is being adequately addressed. If you follow these simple but important recommendations, the risk of developing heart disease can be minimized.

5. CAN I BE CURED OF HIGH BLOOD PRESSURE, DIABETES, OR CHOLESTEROL?

Dr. Capers: A cure means that you no longer have that condition, and you no longer have to be treated for it. High blood pressure, diabetes, and high cholesterol are almost never cured. They can be very successfully treated, however, and kept in check for the rest of your life, by eating healthy, exercising regularly, and taking your medicines as prescribed. I often encounter patients who were prescribed a medication for their hypertension, and it worked: their blood pressure was reduced to a normal range. Then, thinking that they are cured, these patients stopped taking their medications. Of course, the high blood pressure came right back. This is because they weren't *cured* of their high blood pressure; it was just being effectively controlled and treated by medication.

6. DO I NEED A PRIMARY CARE PHYSICIAN?

Dr. Ryan: Yes! Everyone should have a primary care physician. In addition to having someone to turn to when there's a problem, a primary care physician represents your first line of defense against illnesses like heart disease. This is where risk factors can be identified and treated. Primary care physicians can help determine what the likelihood is that you have or might develop heart problems. He or she can also help you devise a treatment plan to prevent this from happening. Most of the prevention strategies that have been discussed in this section are ideally managed through a partnership between you and your primary care physician. If these prevention strategies are not working, or if there are concerns about the presence of heart problems, your primary care physician can refer you to a specialist for further evaluation.

7. OTHER THAN MY ANNUAL DOCTOR'S VISIT, WHEN SHOULD I SEE MY PHYSICIAN?

Dr Capers: You should visit your doctor if you notice something new or different that concerns you. It could be a lump in your breast or a mole on your chin that was not there before, new chest discomfort or shortness of breath, unexplained swelling in the feet and legs, or anything else. If something is concerning you, don't wait until your yearly check up; call your doctor's office and make an appointment. If you are suffering with pain or you are extremely anxious about a new condition and cannot wait until your appointment, don't hesitate to visit the emergency room; that is why they are there.

8. WHAT TESTS SHOULD I REQUEST?

Dr. Ryan: If you are concerned about the possibility of heart disease or if you are at high risk for developing it, talk to you doctor. Make sure you are doing all of the necessary things to prevent the development or progression of heart disease. It's also important to discuss with your doctor whether or not additional testing is appropriate. This is particularly true if you are having symptoms that might be due to a heart problem. A variety of tests are available, but the specific recommendations for each individual depend on many factors. It's up to you and your doctor to decide whether testing is necessary, and if so, which tests are right for you.

9. WHAT TESTS WOULD YOU RECOMMEND TO DIAGNOSE OR RULE OUT HEART DISEASE?

Dr. Capers: Electrical problems of the heart, or heart-rhythm disturbances, are best diagnosed by a simple electrocardiogram, or EKG, which traces on paper the manner in which the electricity is moving through your heart.

A weak or enlarged heart or congestive heart failure is best ruled out with an ultrasound of the heart, called an echocardiogram. This test shows the size, shape, and strength of the heart and also gives a clear view of all four of the heart valves, important structures in the heart that can sometimes be damaged or diseased.

Coronary artery disease, the condition in which the heart's arteries are clogged up with plaque, is best screened for with a stress test, in which the rhythm and images of the heart are monitored while the patient exercises on a treadmill. (Exercise can be simulated by a drug for patients who are unable to exercise because of health problems). There are also several special types of CT scans of the heart that can be very effective to screen for the presence of coronary artery blockages.

The most definitive way to evaluate the heart's arteries is with a cardiac catheterization and coronary angiogram. In this test, a long thin tube is advanced to the heart from the groin, wrist, or arm, and used to inject X-ray dye into the arteries while taking moving pictures.

Probably the best way to gauge the overall health of the heart is a stress test accompanied by some type of imaging, echocardiogram, or nuclear pictures of the heart.

10. IF I HAVE SMOKED FOR MORE THAN TEN YEARS AND THEN QUIT, CAN I DECREASE MY CHANCE OF DEVELOPING HEART DISEASE?

Dr. Ryan: Yes, definitely! Quitting smoking is one of the most effective things that you can do to reduce your chances of developing heart disease. We know that women who smoke are six times more likely to develop heart disease than women who don't. On average, women smokers who develop heart disease do so fourteen years earlier than non-smoking women.

Once you quit smoking, your lungs begin to heal within two months, and over the next several years, the increased risk of heart disease brought on by smoking gradually declines. After several years, your risk of heart disease approaches that of a non-smoker. It's never too late to quit, and the benefits of quitting are substantial.

11. WHAT ARE SOME POTENTIAL WARNING SIGNS OF A HEART ATTACK?

Dr. Capers: The most common symptom of a heart attack is chest discomfort, which is often described as a heavy feeling, or a tightness, squeezing, or pressure. This is often accompanied by shortness of breath, and may be accompanied by sweating, dizziness, nausea, and fainting. This description of heart attack pain is considered "classical" or "typical."

However, there are several "atypical" or not-so-common symptoms of a heart attack, and it turns out that women tend to have relatively more of these atypical symptoms than men. Some of these symptoms include profound fatigue, breaking out in a cold sweat for no apparent reason, upper back pain, a deep-seated ache in the throat or neck, and pain in the arms without chest pain. It is important to know your body, know your usual aches and pains, and trust your body when it tells you, "This is not our typical sore back; something is wrong!"

12. WHAT CAN BE DONE TO KEEP MY ARTERIES CLEAR, HEALTHY, AND OPEN?

Dr. Capers: Diseased arteries that result in a critical reduction in blood supply to the heart and brain are responsible for heart attacks and strokes, respectively; such arteries are affected by a disorder called *atherosclerosis*, where the arteries become clogged with plaque. The main ingredient in this artery-clogging material is cholesterol, a natural form of fat that circulates in the bloodstream. Although all people have cholesterol circulating in their blood, certain conditions cause it to deposit into the walls of the artery, and the clogging process begins.

Conditions that accelerate the process of cholesterol deposition into arteries are high blood pressure, higher than average levels of cholesterol in the blood, diabetes, cigarette smoking, and other genetic conditions. In most people, plaque in the arteries grow slowly over twenty to forty years, until it reaches a critical point, causing circulatory problems in the heart, brain, legs, and elsewhere. We know, for instance, that when we see a fifty-year-old man who has suffered a heart attack diagnosed with several heart arteries severely clogged with plaque, those plaques began growing in his heart when he was fifteen to twenty years old.

To keep arteries clean, healthy, and open, first see a doctor and be tested for diabetes, high blood pressure, and high cholesterol. If you have these conditions, as long as they are aggressively treated, your arteries can still be healthy. Daily exercise is an excellent way to keep your arteries healthy. In addition to helping to control your weight, blood pressure, cholesterol levels, and blood sugar, exercise directly benefits your arteries by causing them to produce healthy substances that overwhelm the unhealthy substances that are also being produced. A heart-healthy diet—one that is rich in fruits, vegetables, and fish, but low in saturated fats (butter, cream) and high-cholesterol foods (fatty pieces of red meat, deep-fried food)—can also help keep arteries clean and clear. And of course, everyone should avoid cigarette smoking.

Nutritional Guide for Healthier Living
David Key of Key Body Fitness

I learned from Todd to take care of my body through exercise and proper nutrition. My method was to follow a proper nutritional guide and do a 30–45 minute cardio workout five days a week, along with strength training at least three days a week, and then taking the other two days to enjoy, my favorite foods. The idea of being able to eat what I want on the weekends motivates me to eat healthy and exercise during the week. I love rewarding myself. I also keep a journal of what I eat, because it really makes a difference when you see your eating pattern and have a record of how much and what you consume. This works for me because it provides self-accountability and awareness about what I eat.

Good-quality nutrition is just as important as exercise. To make the most of your exercise, you must eat the right foods. David Key of Key Body Fitness recommends eating five to six meals per day, and nothing after 8:00 p.m. He also suggests a light cardio workout ten to thirty minutes after your last meal.

Here is a list of healthy foods from which to make your meals.

Proteins	Good Carbohydrates Eaten only before 3:00 PM	Vegetables
Chicken Breast	Sweet Potato	Broccoli
Turkey Breast	Yam	Asparagus
Lean Ground Turkey	Squash	Lettuce
Swordfish	Pumpkin	Cauliflower
Orange Roughy	Steamed Wild or Brown Rice	Green Beans
Haddock	Rice Cake	Mushrooms
Salmon	Oatmeal	Spinach
Tuna	Barley	Tomato
Crab	Beans	Peas
Lobster	Corn	Brussels Sprouts
Shrimp	Strawberries	Artichoke
Top Round Steak	Melon	Cabbage
Top Sirloin Steak	Apple	Celery
Buffalo	Fat Free Yogurt (before 10 a.m.)	Zucchini
Egg Whites or Substitutes	Whole Wheat Bread (before 10 a.m.)	Cucumber
Turkey Bacon or Sausage	Grits	Onion
	Cereal (skim milk before 10 a.m.)	Bell Peppers

LIQUIDS: Drink 75 or more ounces of water every day. It is okay to supplement with Crystal Lite or diet soda. Coffee and tea in moderation, without added sugar.

DO NOT EAT: Sugar, honey, cakes, cookies, muffins, potato chips, candy, donuts, pastries, along with bananas and oranges (which are high-glycemic fruits), crackers, oils, fried foods, fast foods, and so on.

Daphne Bell is turning her personal tragedy into a crusade to make people aware of the importance of knowing their family health history and taking all the steps necessary to combat heart disease, the silent killer.

Daphne is the founder and president of *Keeping TABs on Your Heart*, a non-profit organization she developed after the sudden death of her husband, former NFL player Todd Anthony Bell.

To help further her message, she also serves as spokesperson for the American Heart Association and the Ohio State University Richard M. Ross Heart Hospital in Columbus, Ohio.

The Pain Didn't Kill Me is not only about the importance of knowing one's family health history, but it is also about unlocking one's family secrets—however painful. Essentially, our family history shapes our emotional, spiritual, and physical lives ... whether we know our history or not.

There are so many people who have been with me these past four years, encouraging me when I thought I couldn't go any further. Mom, you are my hero, you passed your inner strength on to me. My siblings—Marie, James, Keith, and Kenneth—thank you for the love. James, you held me up when my will was gone. Anika, you keep me focused. My girls—Edie, Nikol, Melanie, and Margaret—you would not let me lose myself. Thank you for walking through my pain with me.

My sincere gratitude to my Pastor, Bishop Howard Tillman: Your words of counsel and advice carried me. You and first lady Glenneth Tillman are a source of strength and encouragement. Pastor Willie and Kathy Templeton, your kindness covered me. Bishop Sherman Watkins, you keep me laughing. Pastor Mike Reeves, you escorted (I mean *pushed*) me out of my comfort zone. Bishop Mark and Emelda Tolbert, your calls were always right on time. Bishop Ronald and Rose Young, you saw in me what I was unable to see. Bishop Noel Jones, thank you. Bob and Bonnie, friends forever. Richard and Kathy, you came whenever I called. Eric, I appreciate you. Archie, Reva, Sean, Joel, Kevin, and Yahne, I love you much.

To Quinn Capers IV, doctor of interventional cardiology and cardiovascular disease, your willingness to share yourself with others changes and saves lives. Who knew we would work together on this level? You are my champion and my friend. God bless you.

To my editors, Joseph A. Woods and Oriana Leckert, thank you for stepping in at the eleventh hour of my assignment. You took on the task of taking my words which were scattered like a puzzle and pulled them together to make a beautiful picture. Marilyn Foster of Lumen-us Publications, thank you for believing in me.

To my Ohio State University Medical Center partners— Dr. William Abraham, Director, Division of Cardiovascular

Medicine; Dr. John Larry, Associate Clinical Professor; Dr. Subha Raman, Associate Professor of Medicine; Dr. Thomas Ryan, Director, Ohio State Heart Center; Amy Sturm, Certified Genetic Counselor; Larry Anstine, Chief Executive Officer; and Toni Hare, Director, Communications—thank you for embracing my initiative to create awareness about heart disease in the minority community. I appreciate your support and commitment. Jennifer Reimer, you were there from the start.

To Jeff Wilson of Radio One Columbus, you understand and share my mission. Thank you so much.

I give honor to my Lord and Savior Jesus Christ. He is my life and how truly blessed I am that God traded my pain for passion.

THE PAIN DIDN'T *Kill* ME

MY STORY FROM THE HEART

Order additional copies at www.daphnebell.com

Proceeds will go to Keeping TABs on Your Heart, a foundation committed to serving the uninsured and the underserved—particularly those who are diagnosed with *diabetes*, *hypertension*, and/or *cholesterol*—by providing free heart screenings to determine their risk factor for developing heart disease.

For more information or to donate to this cause, go to: www.ktoyh.org